OTHER BOOKS BY LIFE PRESS

Geraldine Ketchum Crow
Bloom Where You Are Transplanted

Elaine Nunnally Davis
Eve's Fruit
The Mothers of Jesus

OTHER BOOKS BY
FRANCES BRINKLEY COWDEN

Etchings Across the Moon
Of Butterflies and Unicorns
View from A Mississippi River Cotton Sack

Cover Art by Fredrick L. Virgous

OUR GOLDEN THREAD

Dealing with Grief
Through Faith

*The butterfly is a perfect symbol of the Resurrection
and the promise it brings to the believer.*

Vanessa virginiensis, American Painted Lady on
Zinnia. Photograph by Neal Hogenbirk

OUR GOLDEN THREAD

Dealing with Grief
Through Faith

Frances Brinkley Cowden

and guest authors from all walks of life
with personal stories and testimonies

Introduction by Dr. Joe E. Piercey

Edited by
Frances Brinkley Cowden
Patricia Smith
Dr. Malra Treece
Marcelle Brinkley Zarshenas

LIFE PRESS
Germantown, Tennessee

Verses marked NIV are scriptures taken from the *HOLY BIBLE, NEW INTERNATIONAL VERSION.* Copyright 1973, 1978, 1984 International Bible Society. Used by permission of Zondervan Bible Publishers.
Verses not marked are from the King James Version of the *Holy Bible.*

Library of Congress Cataloging-in-Publication Data

Cowden, Frances Brinkley.
    Our golden thread : dealing with grief through faith / Frances Brinkley Cowden and guest authors from all walks of life... ; introduction by Joe E. Piercey ; edited by Frances Brinkley Cowden
... [et al .] . -- lst ed.
        p. cm .

        ISBN 1-884289-10-X
        1. Consolation. 2. Bereavement--Religious aspects---Christianity--Miscellanea. 3. Death--Religious aspects--Christianity--Miscellanea. I. Title.
BV4900.C68 1996
242' .4--dc20   96-15972
                                                    CIP
Although the stories represented in this book are based on actual events, some of the names have been changed.

FIRST EDITION: 1996

LIFE PRESS
8463 Deerfield Lane
Germantown, Tennessee 38138

Dedicated to children of God who
support each other in times of grief

OUR GOLDEN THREAD

Love
a golden thread
that cannot be dulled
or broken by time
binds us to each other
and to God
and keeps us
from ever
being
all alone.

--Frances Brinkley Cowden

Life Press prints all books on recycled paper in accordance with the
philosophy of helping to preserve the earth. For the same reason most of
the customary blank pages are omitted.

*Faith is flying upward
like a bird
knowing home is where you are
and where you are going.*

Frances Brinkley Cowden

Laurus argentatus, **Common herring gull,
Photograph by Neal Hogenbirk**

CONTENTS:

OUR GOLDEN THREAD

Reading the entries in this volume one feels privileged to be entering into the very heart and soul of the authors. One finds here the living fabric of which human life and experience are woven. There is indeed a Golden Thread that stitches together the precious patches of joy and sorrow, of pain and celebration, of loss and triumph, that together form the rich and varied fabric of our lives. That Golden Thread is the faithful recognition of God's living presence in our lives.

These vignettes of life and faith reminds one of Psalm 23, especially verse 4 (NIV):

> "Even though I walk through the valley
> of the shadow of death,
> I will fear no evil;
> for you are with me;
> your rod and your staff,
> they comfort me."

These words set forth both the real nature of human experience and the assurance of God's presence. The Psalmist does not say, "If I ever walk through the valley." Rather it is faithfully stated, "Even though I walk through" that difficult valley. Life teaches us that it isn't a matter of "if" but "when" the difficult times of life come to us. For some, they come early and persist; for others, they come late and with finality. But the difficult times do come to all of us.

Yet for all the realism of this recognition of the nature of life, the greatest affirmation is the assurance of God's presence as a force for good and a resource of help: "You are with me; your rod and your staff, they comfort me." This testimony is not about speculative faith in God but the realized presence of God who is with us for comfort and strength.

In ancient times there was a monastery in the area of Gaza. On a wall in the dining room there was a large red dot representing God. Smaller dots were randomly placed around the "God-dot." These represented members of the community as well as their family and friends. Lines were drawn from each small dot to the larger one. The resulting graphic made a very apparent pronouncement: the closer we get to God, the closer we get to each other.

These writings include both the imagery of poetry and the picture-clear details of prose. They are vehicles of grace, bringing us closer to God and closer to each other, uniting us through the Golden Thread of our shared relationship with our gracious God. I sincerely hope you find the blessing in them that I have.

Joe E. Piercey
Senior Pastor
Colonial Park United Methodist Church
Memphis, Tennessee

DENIAL

Job: *"If only my anguish could be weighed
and all my misery be placed on the scales!
It would surely outweigh the sand of the seas--
no wonder my words have been impetuous.
The arrows of the Almighty are in me..."*
Job 6:2-4 (NIV)

God: *"Would you discredit my justice?
Would you condemn me to justify yourself?
Do you have an arm like God's,
and can your voice thunder like his?"*
Job 40:8-9 (NIV)

Christ: *"Simon, Simon, Satan has asked to sift you as
wheat. But I have prayed for you, Simon, that your
faith may not fail. And when you have turned back,
strengthen your brothers."*
Luke 22: 31-32 (NIV)

"In whom the god of this world hath blinded the minds of them which believe not, lest the light of the glorious gospel of Christ, who is the image of God, should shine unto them." II Corinthians 4:4.

IN THE GRIP OF DARK CLAWS

...though your sins be as scarlet, they shall be as white as snow;
Isaiah 1:18

Denial takes many forms. Holding back the tears. Holding on to pain and fear of separation and loss. Defiance. Guilt. None are pleasant. All are crippling and blind us to God's all-powerful Grace.

This book is not about self-help; it is about God's help. A friend of mine who had just lost her husband said, "I can make it because I have faith." She was told, "Faith and grief are two separate things."

In my studies and interviews for this book, I have found that although grief brings pain to the faithful as well as to the faithless, there is a big difference. The longevity and intensity of grief and the scars it leaves are in reverse proportion to where the individual is or comes to be in his walk of faith.

With grief we are brought face to face with our God. More than ever before we have to determine who we are and who God is.

"He has penance done and penance more to do" so said the narrator of the *Rime of the Ancient Mariner.* It is one of the most tragic lines in the history of mankind. To refuse to accept the gift of forgiveness so free for the asking is the saddest and most cruel form of denial. I know. I lived it.

Almost thirty years ago I was involved in a tragedy. Backing out of my driveway onto a county road, I looked into my rear view mirror and saw a motorcycle barreling toward my car from over the hill. I reached for the shift to forward gear. But by the time I had pushed the button, the cycle thundered into the rear of my car. A teenage boy was killed. And I went into a severe depression.

15

But I wadded the pain and guilt into a tight ball and stuffed it into my soul, unable to let go. There was a period of painful searching for answers, rebellion and self-pity.

I could not drive into the driveway without reliving the scene. And my husband did not understand. During that time a faltering marriage dissolved--I and my four small children moved to a larger city. I held on to my self-crucifixion complex year after year, refusing to let go. I wore it like the albatross around my neck that I would not give up.

All I had to do was realize that Christ had already died for me. Reading about John Newton's life as a slave trader and the beautiful discovery of God's "Amazing Grace" made me realize that if God could forgive him and give such a powerful and beautiful song through him, then surely he could forgive me.

Guilt is a phase of grief with the cruelest of dark claws. It is so vital to get released from those claws as soon as possible to prevent scars that could last a lifetime.

Denial is the opposite of trust. I went to church every Sunday. Yet I was an unbeliever because I could not believe that God could forgive me. Until we can give God our guilt, real or imagined, we cannot give him our grief. Suffering can make us scarred or stronger. We can reach inward, curl up and be totally absorbed with self or we can reach outward and accept the love of each other and grow in the understanding of our God. Claws can destroy or claws can dig into the earth and build.

FBC

THE BLINDED HEART

Brad A. Thomas

The ascent to Jerusalem, God upon the colt of an ass. Shouts of, "Hosanna!" to the King.

My heart swelled with joy, my mind racing; pride, like blood, coursed through my veins.

Indeed, I thought, today is now the day of salvation! Today God comes to his temple to judge with justice and righteousness, and I, Peter, walk at his right hand!

My heart swelled with joy, my mind racing; pride, like blood, coursed through my veins.

On to the Temple Mount, the final encounter! A time of judgment is upon the house of Israel, and I, Peter, am the sword in the right hand of the Son of the living God.

My heart swelled with joy, my mind racing; pride, like blood, coursed through my veins.

In the Temple courtyard, tables turned, jealous words were spoken, fools scattered like chaff before the wind, God in his temple at last, and I, Peter, the switch in his right hand!

My heart swelled with joy, my mind racing; pride, like blood, coursed through my veins.

God bent low to wash my dirty feet. "You'll not wash my feet!" said I, heart filled with joy, mind racing; pride, like blood coursed through my veins.

"You'll have no part in me unless you let me wash you," said He. "Then wash all of me," said I, heart filled with joy, mind racing; pride, like blood coursed through my veins.

"This is my body, this is my blood, I die that you might live!" "God forbid, I will die with you!" said I, heart filled with joy, mind racing; pride, like blood coursed through my veins.

The hour was late, he, far off, praying. Sleep heavy upon my head. Startled awake! A mob with torches burning! A traitor, a kiss! Sword drawn to strike a blow for the kingdom!

My heart filled with anger, mind racing; fear, like blood coursed through my veins.

My Lord arrested, friends scattered. Following at a distance, a trial before the Sanhedrin. What has happened to all of our plans for power and glory?

My heart filled with dread, my mind racing; fear, like blood, coursed through my veins.

In the courtyard, a servant girl; "This man was also with him!" "Not me," said I. "You also are one of them." "No, I do not know him!" said I. "Surely this man was also with him, for he is a Galilean!" "Man, I swear by all that I hold sacred, I do not know him!" The echo of denial recedes as the cock's crow pierces the cool, damp morning air.

My heart choked in my throat, mind reeling, weeping, gnashing of teeth, anguish, regret; self-loathing, like blood, coursed through my veins.

Crucifixion ... anguish, death; all hopes and dreams sealed in a tomb.

My heart broken, my mind numb; failure, like blood coursed through my veins.

Resurrection! My heart leapt for joy, mind racing; confusion, like blood, coursed through my veins.

Restoration... "Peter, do you love me?" "Yes, Lord," said I. "Then feed my lambs," said he. "Peter, do you love me?" "Yes, Lord, you know I love you," said I. "Feed my flock," said he. "Peter, do you love me?" "Lord, you know all things, you know that I love you," said I. "Then feed my sheep," said he.

My heart filled with joy, my mind clear; purpose and conviction, like blood, coursed through my veins.

Reverend Brad Thomas is Associate Pastor of Colonial Park United Methodist Church, Memphis, Tennessee

18

SEARCHING FOR ANSWERS

GRAVE SIDE

Cold wind of death
Chills the hearts
Bleak November day
Penetrates to the very bone
Huddled among family and friends
Heavy loneliness overwhelms
Comforting words are spoken
Eulogy is given
Warmth slowly calms gives peace
Bright sunshine of love
Pours from the grave

He is not gone
Through us, he lives.

Frances Darby

Have mercy on me, O God, have mercy on me, for in you my soul takes refuge. I will take refuge in the shadow of your wings until the disaster has passed.
Psalm 57:1 (NIV)

MEDITATIONS ON GRIEF

Life passes like a comet - a broad swoop,
then the inevitable fall.
Trying to conjure up past fleeting ecstasies and dwelling on
them remains difficult.
Mind games rampant with traumas and tragedies. In
need of control.
Caring allays emotional affliction.
Helping hands - -
A smile, a touch, a welcome call
Sincere
These gestures say it all!
It is at these tragic times that one's faith in the Superior
Force
affords comfort and wisdom to accept the greatest of losses.

Rita Lurie

A free-lance writer, Rita Lurie is coordinator of a senior
citizens writing group at East Center, at Gaisman, Memphis,
Tennessee

ENTREATY

These demons took away my second son:
Lust, Marijuana, Alcohol, Cocaine...
Their name is Legion; mine is only one.
Lord, be at hand. Let not the Darkness reign.

The years before he knew me took their toll:
Try though I did, I could not salve his pain
Nor fill the void that loomed within his soul.
Lord, be at hand. Let not the Darkness reign.

Christ, give your bearer strength to bear his cross.
To his small brother can he yet explain
Why we, a second time, endure this loss?
Lord, be at hand. Let not the Darkness reign.

Love still abides, but no more false belief:
I know he cannot live with us again,
Healer, guide us to life beyond the grief.
Lord, be at hand. Let not the Darkness reign!

Vassar W. Smith
Pal Alto, California

This poem was originally published in The Plowman anthology, *Morning At East Elementary School,* 1990 and *The Serious Side* by Vassar Smith, © 1990, The Plowman Press.

THE SILENT NIGHT

The silent night
has come again.
There is no sound
but slowly dripping rain.

The rain keeps coming
like silent tears.
Will it wash away
all our troubled years?

The dawn is here
finally, at last.
The rain's gone too
for a final rest.

Oh Justice, where are you?
Behold your sting!
The storm clouds pass,
and the birds on wing.

How silently we pray,
in glad gratitude
that we survived
another storm without you.

Violet Latham
March 19, 1984

Violet and Glenn Latham went through a horrifying experience when their teenage son Wayne was killed by a drunk driver. In a twist of justice the driver was given probation, and they had to go through bankruptcy and move on.

In her book, *Justice or Mercy*, she states that "Our guiding light through our tragedy is our favorite Bible selection, Ecclesiastes 3:1-15. *To everything there is a season and a time to every purpose under the Heaven...*"

Violet Latham goes on to say:

"Perhaps forgiving the young man who had done this, someday, would be our last memorial to him [Wayne]. Someday, God will make it clear to all of us the purpose of our tragedy....we try to comfort others who have gone through a similar situation."

The Lathams now live in Fayetteville, Arkansas, and are members of Colbaugh First Baptist Church, Hindsville, Arkansas.

"....and call upon me in the day of trouble; I will deliver you and you will honor me." Psalm 50:15 (NIV)

FROM OUT OF THE DARKNESS

In memory of Gladys Louise Bullard--1901-1992

In times of sorrow even a poet has difficulty finding the words that will heal and comfort. I had tried talking to friends, going through my grandmother's pictures, writing poems about her and crying. I even prayed every time I went to church, but nothing seemed to ease my since of loss. My grandmother had been gone from this earth for six months before I had a prayer experience that was to change my life and eventually lead to the publication of this book, *Our Golden Thread.*

I slipped out of bed very early one morning--grief made sleep impossible. Although I had grandchildren of my own, I had been unable to resolve my grandmother's death. Everything reminded me of her: the dishcloths she had bought me the last time I took her shopping; the chair she had sat in last Easter, the last time she had been in my home, then surrounded by great grandchildren and great-great grandchildren. We had made photographs of the five generations including my mother and myself and each of my children and their children. I know she got tired of all the picture taking. Even my dad complained that the children's eyes would be permanently damaged from the camera flashing. But she sat holding great-great grandchildren, smiling for the camera each time I asked her to.

I had been depressed because she had been put into the nursing home two years prior to her death. However, she had adjusted quite well herself. She hobbled around with her walker, cheering up everyone who was well enough to enjoy her conversation. She tried in every way to make herself as useful as possible. But it broke my heart every time I visited the tiny gray room that she had filled with a few mementos from her long and loving life.

Her last fateful summer she began having problems with her heart and became very weak. When she realized that she would never be well enough to leave her bed except in a wheelchair, she willed herself to leave the physical world. She got rid of her telephone and her television and gave back almost everything in the room to the loved ones who had given them to her, or to others if that was not possible. When she died, almost everything in her room was gone except a very few photographs, a framed copy of the prayer of St. Francis of Assisi, and her Bible. I never resolved her being in a nursing home, so I certainly had yet to resolve myself to her death.

I could not begin to resolve my grief until I truly put it in God's hands. "I just cannot stand it," I had finally prayed. "Please, help me!"

Then after much prayer and tears, I experienced a wonderful overflowing of the Holy Spirit. Phrases from hymns and scripture came to me and I experienced a joy and peace I had never known. I found a new focus for my life.

A few weeks later, I was writing a poem about the experience. I wrote three pages, going into great detail about the patterns of light the moon etched into the darkness through the lace curtains and the great joy that I had experienced. I finished the poem with an image that suggested that although I still did not know the answer to the "why" I had asked at the beginning of the poem, I was resolved that the world needed Grandma much more than Grandma needed the world. Yet, I still had not completely resolved my grief.

I decided to move the poem to another document. I copied what I thought was the entire three pages. But something strange happened on the computer. After my "cut" and "paste" was completed, only three words were transported to the new document. "**Loss   revealed love.**" But those three words said it all.

I did not try to undo my cutting or go back to try to recreate the poem. I realized that God had given me the answer to "why." It had been buried in the three-page poem until it was singled out. I have still not figured out how a "cut-paste" command could have pulled words from the middle of the document and deleted everything else. But I understand why. From out of the darkness came a small miracle, a wonder as ancient as points of light from the moon, and as modern as the electronic age where even man-made handiwork is not immune to a touch from the finger of God.

FBC

Yea, though I walk through the valley of the shadow of death, I will fear no evil; for thou art with me; thy rod and thy staff, they comfort me. Psalm 23:4.

"THE VALLEY OF THE SHADOW OF DEATH"

I asked a friend to write about dealing with the loss of a loved one through suicide. She said she would try. "But it will be hard," she explained. "No loss is more devastating. But we can't judge what took place in those final moments. We don't know what happened between our merciful Lord and His child just before death."

I had a former student who shot herself in the head and then decided she wanted to live. Although blinded by pain and blood, she was able to get help; and, luckily, she lived. Others might have made that decision to no avail. We do not know. We are not to know. We are only to know that there is a God of Love that we can always depend upon.

FBC

PULLING OUT OF
SELF PITY

Save me from all my transgressions;
do not make me the scorn of fools.
I was silent; I would not open my mouth,
for you are the one who has done this.
Remove your scourge from me;
I am overcome by the blow of your hand.
You rebuke and discipline men for their sin;
you consume their wealth like a moth--
each man is but a breath.

"Hear my prayer, O LORD,
listen to my cry for help;
be not deaf to my weeping.
For I dwell with you as an alien,
a stranger, as all my fathers were.
Look away from me, that I may rejoice again
before I depart and am no more.

Psalm 39:8-13 (NIV)

You have made my days a mere handbreadth;
the span of my life is nothing before you.
Each man's life is but a breath.
Psalm 39:5 (NIV)

A CURE FOR SELF PITY:
A LOOK AT PSALM 39

Martha McNatt

Occasionally I lapse into a mood of self pity. I am overworked. I feel the futility of my efforts to be a good homemaker, mother, and career woman. Constant demands are made upon my time, my strength, and my brain power. "Poor Me," I moan, "I push myself to exhaustion and nobody cares." I wallow in self pity.

When I exert extra effort to be productive, my superiors respond by giving me additional work to do. I feel the futility of my efforts to be a good homemaker. I work hard to provide a clean and wholesome environment for my family. They often react with muddy footprints, dog hairs, and shoes kicked under the sofa.

I taxi children to ball practice, flute lessons, and Cub Scouts. I go to P. T. A. meetings and parent conferences. I bake cookies for the class parties and drive for field trips. I am rewarded with more demands upon my time and my skills.

The writer of Psalm 39 also experienced self pity. A comforting thought is the fact that David, King of Israel, who had everything--riches, power, fame, and strength, experienced some of the same feelings that I do.

In the Psalm, he moans about the futility of bustling about. He muses about the brevity of life, and the rebukes he suffers from the hand of God. *The Living Bible* translates his prayer in these words. "Hear my prayer, Oh, Lord, for I am your guest. Let me be filled with happiness again." These words, I have stored in my prayer bank. When I am stressed to the breaking point, unappreciated, exhausted and

surrounded by a mountain of dirty laundry, I remember
David, and I pray:
"Hear my prayer, Oh Lord, for I am your guest. Let me
recover and be filled with happiness again."

From the forthcoming, *A Collection of Meditations for
Women in the Workplace,* by Martha McNatt, a free-lance
writer from Humbolt, Tennessee. She is a member of First
Christian Church, Jackson, Tennessee.

PEARS, PRAYERS AND POND WATER

Based on a news story, *Jackson Sun*, Jackson, TN

Martha McNatt

Tears welled up in Evelyn's eyes and dripped from under her glasses. She wiped a wisp of gray hair from her seventy-five-year-old face and dabbed her eyes with the tail of the long shirt that hung loosely over her one-hundred-pound frame. She was having a terrible day. It was the third anniversary of the death of her husband of more than forty years.

As she reached into the refrigerator to prepare herself a snack, Evelyn saw a jar of pear honey, a homemade delicacy of ground pears, sugar, and lemon slices. Evelyn spooned a bit on a saltine and nibbled it, remembering an aging pear tree in a field not far from her rural home.

"Later today I might check on this year's pear crop." she mused aloud. "I might make a new batch of pear honey, for the girls, if the cows haven't stripped the tree."

The mid-afternoon sun beamed hot as Evelyn started in search of the pear tree. Across the road, and into a field of soybeans, Evelyn walked. Her face soon began to perspire and briars tore at the legs of her worn cotton pants.

"That old tree should be just about here." she thought. Evelyn retraced her steps--or so she thought--but the pear tree was nowhere in sight, "I feel like Dumb Dora," she said aloud, "I know that tree is around here some place."

She walked the field from end to end and crisscrossed one side to the other, with the same result. "Maybe a storm blew the tree down," Evelyn reasoned. "I'll just give up. The road is across that wooded lot. I will just go home and forget it."

The wooded area seemed larger than she remembered, but Evelyn kept walking. She could hear road traffic, but it seemed far away and she began to feel very tired. Suddenly the woods ended, and there ahead of her was not the road, but a three-strand barbed wire fence, and across the fence was a field of yellow bitter weeds and scrubby grass.

Holding down the bottom strand of wire with her size-five sneaker, Evelyn bent her slight frame to squeeze between the wires. Suddenly her foot slipped and a rusty barb slashed a six-inch gash through her pants and into her leg just above the ankle. Blood streamed from the cut and ran into her shoe.

"Now I've done it," she muttered, and reached into her pocket for a tissue. Finding none, she sat on the ground and wiped the blood with her long shirt tail. The cut was bleeding freely, Evelyn tore a strip from the tail of her shirt and folded it into a bandage for the cut. Sitting very still, she held the bandage with her hands until the blood clotted and dried, coating her hands with a brown sticky mess.

"I've got to get out of here," she told herself. "I have had enough exercise for one day." Completing her first-aid treatment, Evelyn pulled herself to her feet and headed once again for the bean field. The beans were higher than her head. She began walking across the bean rows, but her leg hurt and the fuzzy leaves made her skin burn. She trudged on, step after weary step, but the road did not appear.

For the first time, Evelyn admitted she was lost, The sun was sinking behind the trees as she headed once again for the wooded area. Hot and exhausted, she sank to the ground, leaned against a tree and prayed, "Now Lord, I got me into this mess. Looks like it is up to you to get me out of it. I'll keep walking, Lord, but from now on, you be the navigator. I don't know which way to go. I don't know which way is straight up."

Evelyn felt suddenly peaceful--unafraid but very tired. She began to pull together a pile of leaves and grass for a pillow, Finally she pulled her shirt tightly around her body and slept. During the night she was aware of the buzzing of insects, and the sting of mosquitoes that attacked her exposed face, hands and ankles.

When daylight appeared, Evelyn awakened to an extreme thirst. A light dew lay on the vegetation. She moistened her hands on the wet grass and rubbed her scratched face and her parched lips. She closed her eyes and remembered her husband's face. He often laughed at her when she got into a jam. "Now don't you laugh at me," she told him, and suddenly serious she continued, "One thing I know. I must find some water, or I will not be around very long!"

Every muscle ached as she pulled her small body to her feet. Her leg was stiff and sore, and the dried blood had matted on the makeshift bandage. "If it bleeds again, I will just have to tear off more shirt tail." Evelyn smiled. "Won't I be pretty if I walk in home with my shirt tail torn off just under my chin?"

Not really knowing which way to walk, she came to the edge of the woods. She looked carefully in every direction. Suddenly her spirits lifted. Not far to her right was a farm pond in an open field. She crossed the fence again, this time without mishap, and walked toward the pond. The water was murky; and green slime grew around the edge, but she did not care. The wetness soothed her parched throat and washed away the dried blood from her hands. "Thank you, Lord," she gurgled, warm water streaming down her face onto her tattered shirt.

Near the pond was a scrubby tree. Evelyn sat down in its shade to devise a plan. She decided to declare the pond her headquarters and walk in one direction as far as she dared, returning to the pond if she failed to find a familiar landmark. In spite of her resolve, she spent most of the next two days and nights lying on the ground near the pond. Weak from hunger, her frail body was too tired to respond to her urging. She drank pond water when thirst became unbearable and waited quietly for someone to find her.

On the third day, Evelyn saw a helicopter flying in a giant circle around her. She shouted and waved, with no response from the craft. "They are looking for me." She told herself. For the first time, she allowed herself to think of the pain her family must be feeling. "They think I'm dead," she whispered.

She was right. By the time darkness fell the first day, neighbors had discovered she was missing. When her daughters arrived and found their Mother's doors unlocked, they feared the worst. Had she been kidnapped? Was she lying somewhere dying with a heart attack or a broken hip? Or had she yielded to despondence and taken her own life?

As time passed, hopes grew dimmer for the survival of the missing woman. By the third night, the entire community joined the search. They were looking for her body.

With the third sunset, Evelyn renewed her resolve. Tomorrow she would get those weary bones working and, with the Lord's help, would find her way home. She slept in snatches under her tree. She was cold, and once she heard a snake or a rabbit in the grass near her head.

As soon as the sun rose, Evelyn began to move around. Somehow she did not feel as sore today. She did not feel hungry, only weak and a little dizzy. Trying to get her bearings from the morning sun, Evelyn determined that she needed to travel eastward. Taking one last drink of pond water, she faced the sun and started walking. She had walked only a short distance when she saw in the weeds ahead of her, a large soft drink bottle. "That old bottle might save my life," she said. "I could survive a whole day on that much water." Returning to the pond, she washed the dirt from the bottle, and filled it with the murky water, whispering a prayer.

Some of her strength returned as Evelyn walked, keeping her eyes on a post or a tree to avoid walking in circles. Across fields and around fences she walked, listening, watching, praying. Suddenly the sound of an engine came to her ears--like the motor of a truck. It came closer, then stopped. Keeping her eyes on the spot from which the sound came, Evelyn forced her weak legs to approach a row of tall bushes.

She heard another sound--a car door slammed. Still holding her bottle of pond water, she pushed her way through the bushes and there in an open field was a man gathering hay. She did not recognize him, but she hurried toward him to ask for help. When the man saw her, he came running. "I know who you are," he shouted.

The next few hours were a blur. Evelyn was about four miles from home and traveling in the wrong direction. The farmer drove her home. Through laughter, tears, and prayers of thanksgiving, the spunky woman told her story. One of her granddaughters was sobbing. "Why are you crying?" grinned Evelyn. "You found me."

Two days in the hospital, plenty of good food, and several days as the center of attention and Evelyn was as good as new. She would never be the same. During her ordeal she came to grips with the reality of a simple faith in God. When it was over, her strongest emotion was joy in being alive. She was no longer despondent or sorry for herself. She now finds happiness in her faith, her home and her family. Her sense of humor, which had not been visible for three years, has returned. "Mama is again fun to be around." said her daughter.

SAVED BY THE LOVE OF GOD AND A FRIEND NAMED HUGO

Amy Lyn Bellairs

There exists a deep sadness that can drape over a human heart like a blackened shroud, watering the seeds of despair and destroying the precious desire to go on living.

It begins in the depths of the inner person as fingers of pain wrap themselves around a starved and naked soul. A tiny voice whispering in the dark proclaims the absence of self-worth, sparking and fueling the fires of futility.

In solemn solitude, the festering mass that was once the warm heart of a believer grows colder, day after day.

I know this place. I have known that draping depression and felt its subtle suffocation. Thoughts of permanent escape occupied my mind and suicide loomed overhead as the ultimate solution.

Thankfully, the warm goofy smile of a Guatemalan friend named Hugo cast a beam of hope into my heart just in time. His English was fair, and my Spanish was bad; but somehow, the message of Love broke through.

Hugo's tawny face fairly glowed with the love of God and he shared with me, in his broken English, the joy he carried within his heart. Although I had experienced salvation in my youth, the cold reality of lingering loneliness and sorrowful solitude had captured the very life of my soul. Hugo gently reminded me that I was God's child. In simple phrases, he assured me I was loved by my Creator and had been created for a purpose. I listened to him, believing his words eagerly. I heard the voice of God through the words of my special friend.

The love of the Almighty God shattered my sadness and ripped apart the dark shrouds of deep despair. My hungry heart leaped for joy once more and the thoughts of ending what God himself had begun were chased away like shadows dispelled by a candle's light. God's love dwelled anew within and I began to fully understand, truly "how wide and long and high and deep is the love of Christ." Ephesians 3:18 (NIV)

Amy Bellairs is a new mother, writer and homemaker. She is active in the Oak Grove Baptist Church in Joplin, Missouri, where she and her husband James live.

THE MESSENGER

This testimony of faith happened to me in 1979. It was such an overwhelming experience that it was nearly fifteen years before I was ready to write about it, although I have shared the story verbally with many people.

Shirley Rounds Schirz

With no strength left to even reach for my buzzer, I watched the seconds tick away on the clock and prayed, "Will you do something to help me, Lord?" Verses from James wove themselves like gold thread through my prayers: "And the prayer of faith shall save the sick, and the Lord shall raise them up." (James 5:15) "... but let him ask in faith, nothing wavering..." (James 1:6)

My eyes moved slightly at the sound of my hospital room door swinging open and closed, but I was unable to respond.

"I said, is it okay if I stay in here for a while?" a voice asked.

Fever had made me slip in and out of consciousness for the past hour, but even with blurred vision I could see his black robe. "I'm not a Catholic, Father," I whispered with the only voice I could muster.

"I know you're not Catholic. There would be a cross beside your door in the hallway if you were. They do that so I know where to stop to offer the sacraments."

He moved to my window, standing so his profile blocked the late afternoon sun. I struggled to remain conscious. It seemed strange that he had appeared in my room.   An hour before, I had given up trying to raise enough strength to reach my buzzer or to call out. I had prayed that God would send someone in, and, now, here someone stood. Certainly, God had sent him.

Before I could ask him to hand me my buzzer or go get me a nurse, he moved to stand over me. Desperation etched his face with a sadness, a grief so heavy that it seemed to be pulling his jowls downward. "Can I, please, just stay in here a minute?"

"Why do you want to stay in here?"

Without moving his head, his voice as distant as his gaze, he said, "Because no one will look for me in here, and I don't want to be found right now."

I wanted to ask why he was hiding, but my ears rang, the room spun. I needed for him to get me some help, but I accepted that God had sent him. I would be all right, soon. I lay back, letting him evaporate from view as my life slipped a little farther away.

Suddenly, his sobs awakened me. I felt alert, stronger. "What's wrong? Why are you crying? What are you hiding from?"

His shoulders shook, and he dropped into the armchair where my brother had sat hours before. I squinted, wanting to see my brother Skip sitting there. Surely, he would have gotten me a nurse by then. Someone needed to know I was dying.

But, the blurry image in the chair beside me wasn't Skip. He had said he wouldn't be back that night. In fact, I wasn't expecting any visitors my third night of lying in pain, dying.

No one had been in for hours, not even the nurses. It was Sunday late afternoon. When the shifts had changed hours before, a spunky, short nurse had popped her head in to say she'd be back. I tried to summon her, but she rushed away. She hadn't come back.

They were all busy with the poor woman in the room next to mine, the room where policemen had stood guard all night and that morning until her husband had been arrested--the room where I had heard them wheel her in and out four times in the night to do emergency surgeries.

41

Voices had been just outside my door when they brought her back each time. They had performed eye surgery to save her right eye, after two limb amputations to clean up the jagged edges her husband had left behind. As the police talked, I learned her story.

Her husband had tortured her, cutting off two fingers first, then one leg below the knee. He had stabbed her numerous times, and cut out one eye. By the time she was rescued, there was little hope of saving her. As I heard of these horrors, I cried for her. And then I prayed. I prayed for her each time I woke up during the night and continued to pray for her and her doctors as Sunday wore on. By the time my brother Skip had come and gone and the shifts had changed, she was resting comfortably, the police guards gone--her husband apprehended somewhere in Wisconsin.

Only then did I realize no one had been in to examine me since Saturday at 6 a.m. I began to pray for my own life. Early Sunday morning, my blood had been drawn, and an intern had stopped in to read my chart, saying my white count was high and that a doctor would be in later. None came. I had given up hope of ever seeing another living soul---until the priest arrived.

His shoulders shook. Gasping sobs escaped his throat. The man was suffering. *He's lost someone he loved.* Certain that was it, I asked him, "Did you just lose someone?"

The sudden upward jerk of his head would have startled me, except my body was drained beyond adrenaline rushes. Anger reddened his wet face.

"Lose someone? I've lost everyone! My whole parish! They took my church away and gave me this hospital! And I don't want to be here!"

His outburst roused me, his confession striking a chord of sympathy.

"But you can do good work here," I whispered, fighting to keep my eyes open.

God, give me the strength to help this man, so he can help me.

"Like what? Last rites? I came here to do that when I had my church. Now I have nothing. No weddings, no baptisms, nothing but pain and misery and last rites!"

I felt myself slipping away. Somewhere in the hollow of a long, dark tunnel, his sobs echoed like the soft, steady drumming of ocean waves. I completely forgot that I had been lying in that bed since Friday night, admitted with stomach pains that we thought were a reaction to pills my husband and I had taken to prevent us from getting sick from Mexican water.

We had been on our way to O' Hare when what I had noticed as cramps at noon turned into screaming pain by 9 p.m.

"Take me to the hospital!" I had begged my husband when we were outside Beloit.

"If you can wait a half hour, we'll be in Rockford." The thought of being in my hometown encouraged me to keep the screams down, bite my tongue and cry into the crook of my arm the next half hour, rocking in a tight fetal position.

When we got to the emergency room, I couldn't stand upright. Tom went in ahead of me to get help, and I stumbled toward the glass doors. I wanted in. I wanted someone to make the pain stop. Two nurses and two orderlies maintained their relaxed stances by a counter. When Tom blurted out that we'd taken some drug, they misunderstood and made no effort to move. Even with my body bent in half, I caught a glimpse of the knowing looks that passed between them. Smirks, almost as if to say, "A druggie, huh? Well, let her suffer."

Tom asked where he could lay me down. They told him to go get the bottle of pills from his suitcase, and one nurse led the way to an examining room while I struggled behind, unassisted.

A half hour later, the doctor on-call arrived. He'd been at a party, he said, and his breath smelled of alcohol. He gave me something to kill the pain, and I slipped drowsily off to sleep. When I woke, I had been admitted,

the doctor had told Tom to go ahead to O' Hare Airport
and use his non-refundable ticket, that the hospital would
arrange to get me to O' Hare for the next flight out on
Saturday.

I knew a bus ran to the airport so I lay back and
slept, willing myself to heal quickly, praying that the effects
of the drug would move out of my body. We were
celebrating our tenth anniversary with a trip to Cozamel,
and I wanted desperately to be there with Tom. I reasoned
I would feel fine once the pill wore off. But I didn't, and by
morning my white blood cell count had soared.

"Some kind of infection. We'll watch you yet
today," an assigned doctor had said on Saturday morning at
6 a.m. That was the last doctor I was to see.

My brother and sisters visited me throughout the
day Saturday. Each of them had spoken to the nurses; each
nurse assured them that everything was being done for me.
Then the tortured woman had arrived, and everyone else on
the floor became secondary to her nightmare.

I opened my eyes one last time and saw the tear-
stained face of the broken-hearted priest. Didn't he realize
how much people here needed him? "...be ye doers of the
word, and not only hearers..." (James 1:22)

Raising my head slightly, reaching deep within for
strength that was no longer my own, praying for my Lord
to help me, I said, "This hospital needs you."

"Anyone could be a hospital priest. I am good with
a parish, with families, with counseling and births and
weddings."

His voice broke, his spirit gone.

"You can counsel here. You can give comfort to
people who really need it. The poor woman in the next
room needs you." He was listening, which gave me
courage to go on. "And you know, it's when people need
God that you can lead them to salvation. Here, you will
have the opportunity to lead souls to Jesus every day, while
in your parish you had a whole church full of people who'd
already been led."

My head sunk back on my pillow. My time had come. My eyes met his and his countenance brightened. A smile edged his lips after he wiped his tears on a floppy sleeve.

He reached down and took my hand. "I can't believe God sent you to me."

I smiled as my eyes closed. "I think He sent you to me."

He squeezed my hands in both of his. "May I bless you?"

When he finished, he asked, "Is there anything I can do for you?" Once again I gathered strength to whisper, my eyes heavy, the tunnel dark and narrow. "Could you get me a doctor? I'm dying."

I heard him rush from the room. It didn't matter then how fast any of them moved. I was at peace. God would take care of me.

I drifted into unconsciousness.

Days later, I was the talk of the hospital--how I had lived for forty-five hours with a ruptured appendix, how my husband had called from Cozamel Sunday night only to learn I was in emergency surgery fighting for my life, how the doctor had estimated that I'd had less than fifteen minutes to live when he operated, a short twelve minutes after the priest left my room.

There were a lot of mouths saying "Unbelievable!" and "Miraculous!" that week, and they were right. It was God, plain and simple, using me to win back a servant, using that servant to save my life. Yes, it was a miracle, as only the hand of God can direct one.

The priest visited me several times during the following week, saying he was busy every minute and was now truly happy in his new calling as hospital chaplain. When he left the first time, he had paused at my feet saying, "I'm going next door now to visit that poor woman you mentioned."

I grinned at him. "Does she have a cross on her door?"

He let a knowing laugh escape his lips. "No, but then, neither did you."

I knew then that God would use him well, that his heart would lead him in his work. We had witnessed first hand what I suspect we both already knew: God is always with us, and faith in that will see us through.

Shirley Rounds Schirz, Fennimore, Wisconsin, is author of *Ashes to Oak*, a Grandmother Earth Creations, 1994 Chapbook Winner. She is deaconess at Trinity Evangelical Free Church and is active in several Christian organizations, including the Friendship Bible Coffees and the Fellowship of Christian Athletes.

LEANING
ON THE PROMISES

Peace I leave with you; my peace I give you. I do not give to you as the world gives. Do not let your hearts be troubled and do not be afraid. John 14:27 (NIV)

So do not fear, for I am with you; do not be dismayed, for I am your God. I will strengthen you and help you; I will uphold you with my righteous right hand. Isaiah 41:10 (NIV)

The salvation of the righteous comes from the Lord; he is their stronghold in time of trouble. Psalm 37:39 (NIV)

For everything that was written in the past was written to teach us, so that through endurance and the encouragement of the Scriptures we might have hope. Romans 15:4 (NIV)

Praise be to the God and Father of our Lord
Jesus Christ, the Father of compassion and the
God of all comfort, who comforts us in all our
troubles, so that we can comfort those in any trouble
with the comfort we ourselves have received from God.
2 Corinthians 1:3,4 (NIV)

WITH CERTAINTY

He knew he must let go;
she was so frail
and suffered in the throe
of pain and agony.
He read her silent plea
to end this long travail.

"Do not fear," she had said,
before she had
been mutely trapped in bed;
"God is our help and strength
whatever span or length
of life, so don't be sad."

He knew that she believed
and was at peace,
though he was sorely grieved.
But, as he felt her slip
from his life's fragile grip,
his fear and doubting ceased.

Barbara Longstreth-Mulkey

A free lance writer and editor of *Tradition,* a poetry
magazine, Mrs. Mulkey is a member of Pulaski Heights
United Methodist Church, Little Rock, Arkansas.

MY GRANNY

As I see your frail little body
I remember how strong it used to be.
I start having flashbacks of you and me
remembering the times we spent together
sitting on your lap as a little girl--
Really, just beginning in my little world
You were already pretty far into yours.
Yet now when I look back,
we were both just little girls
One maybe a few years younger,
one a few years older.
Granny, over the years,
I have felt your pain, sorrow,
sadness and your joy.
I truly understand
and love you with all my heart .

Deborah F. King

"This was written for my grandmother as she was dying.
She had a stroke and died a slow death. My grandmother
had a sad life. We were close because I was very loving to
her. I accepted her with her faults. I loved her and I know
that God loves us both." D. F. King, Corinth, Mississippi, is
a member of Waldron Street Christian Church.

IN THE WORD

When I first started searching for scriptures for this book I found only a few in the concordance of my Bibles. However, the more I studied, the more I discovered that all of the Bible is a story of God's promises to be with and to comfort his people.

I started asking my friends to share the scriptures that had encouraged them in times of grief. Some of them agreed to share their experiences. I am grateful for the testimonies of my friends and family, especially my church family at Colonial Park United Methodist Church. After I realized that I could not write the book without the help of others, I wanted a book that revealed the thoughts of Christians from all walks of life, not just professional writers or scholars. I asked people to write as the Holy Spirit moved me to ask them, praying that they would be led by the Holy Spirit as they wrote.

It took great courage and faith to write in such a personal way for publication. But these Christian friends realizing that their testimonies might encourage others wanted to share how God's love had strengthened them in times of great need.

In addition to the scripture verses in other selections, I am including additional verses here that reveal God's love and **His promise of comfort that every one can claim by faith.** If you pray with a specific one in mind each day, He will deliver joy and peace in the midst of sorrow. Moreover, as you study the word, you will be able to add many more to this list. Copy favorites on small index cards and put them in your wallet or purse. Post them on your bathroom mirror and on the refrigerator; but above all, paste them in your heart.

FBC

The following texts are from the New International Version of *The Holy Bible*:

The eternal God is thy refuge, and underneath are the everlasting arms. Deuteronomy 33:27

Those who know your name will trust in you, for you, Lord, have never forsaken those who seek you. Psalm 9:10

The angel of the Lord encamps around those who fear him, and he delivers them. Psalm 34:7

I waited patiently for the Lord; he turned to me and heard my cry. He lifted me out of the slimy pit, out of the mud and mire; he set my feet on a rock and gave me a firm place to stand. Psalm 40:1, 2

As a father has compassion on his children, so the Lord has compassion on those who fear him; for he knows how we are formed, he remembers that we are dust. Psalm 103:13, 14

You will keep in perfect peace him whose mind is steadfast, because he trusts in you. Isaiah 26:3

The Lord is good, a refuge in times of trouble. He cares for those who trust in him. Nahum 1:7

The Lord your God is with you, he is mighty to save. He will take great delight in you, he will quiet you with his love, he will rejoice over you with singing. Zephaniah 3:17

You will keep in perfect peace him whose mind is steadfast, because he trusts in you. Isaiah 26:3

"I have told you these things, so that in me you may have peace. In this world you will have trouble. But take heart! I have overcome the world." John   16:33

Jesus said to me, "My grace is sufficient for you, for my power is made perfect in weakness.". . . That is why, for Christ's sake, I delight in weaknesses, in insults, in hardships, in persecutions, in difficulties. For when I am weak, then I am strong. 2 Corinthians 12:9, 10

My God will meet all your needs according to his glorious riches in Christ Jesus. Philippians 4:19

"...because the Lord disciplines those he loves, and he punishes everyone he accepts as a son."
"No discipline seems pleasant at the time, but painful. Later on, however, it produces a harvest of righteousness and peace for those who have been trained by it."
Hebrews 12:6, 11

HIS GIFT OF PEACE

Christine Counce

Being able to handle situations where extreme stress and grief are problems is one of today's most sought-after accomplishments. Despondency from grief or loneliness is a major factor in the lives of many people.

God has promised us that, if we will trust Him, He will be with us to see us through whatever comes into our lives. We hear the expression, or promise, of "peace that passes understanding," in our ministers' sermons. We read about it in our Bibles and hear others speak about it, but we cannot quite grasp the true meaning of it until we experience it ourselves. Then we want to tell the world about the wonder of it.

The first time I can recall being definitely aware of this promised peace was when my daddy died. I had always felt that the loss of a parent--one so dear and important in my life--would be more devastating than I could handle. He died the day before Father's Day in 1964.

That night, after falling asleep for a few hours, I awoke and was shocked that I had gone to sleep so peacefully and thought "I went to sleep and my dad is dead!"

I knew in my heart as I sat by his bed on the day that he died, holding his hand, that my dad was going to die before the day was over. Once he turned to me and said, "Take good care of your mother." I just smiled and nodded, because I knew he was assured that his request would be carried out.

I tried to think of what I needed to say to him in these last hours. He already knew how much I loved him. I just kept on holding his hand...all day...until my family insisted that I must leave to get something to eat. I knew he would die while I was gone, so I went very reluctantly.

About halfway through the meal the phone rang and I just knew he had died even though my brother tried to soften the blow by saying, "Daddy is getting worse so you need to come back to the hospital." I felt that God had meant to spare me the pain of seeing the agony of his death.

On the way back to the hospital I began to think about how my mother depended on him so totally during their fifty years of marriage--how lost and afraid she would feel and that I must get to her and hold her and assure her.

Then I thought about our three children, who adored their Gramp so very much and the sadness and loss they would feel and how I would try to explain to them to help them accept such a new situation.

My two sisters then came into my thoughts--one was divorced and the other was not married--they depended and relied on our dad's advice and help. I must try to ease their pain of such a loss.

God works in wondrous ways. In trying hard to make his death easier for those I loved, I had little time to think about what effect it had on me...and I went to sleep that night because God had let me experience the peace that can come, in the midst of deep sorrow, and it defies all understanding!

After having experienced that peace, I realized that I needed to keep trying to reassure others that God will also give that peace to them as the need arises. There are always people who need us and in trying to help them, our own burdens are lifted and become lighter. God helps me in this way.

Christine Counce is Prayer Group Leader of Colonial Park United Methodist Church, Memphis, Tennessee.

A MESSAGE FROM AN ANGEL

Geraldine Ketchum Crow

I awoke from a restless sleep dazed and confused. Beside my bed appeared an angel. Her head and wings were illuminated as she gently swayed back and forth. Then I moved about and felt the piercing pain tear down the center of my chest and radiate to both sides. That brought me to my senses.

Two metallic, helium-filled balloons, a gift from my granddaughter, were tied to a chair at the left of my bed. The round balloon's message was: "Get well soon." The heart-shaped balloon read: "You're the greatest." Air currents had eased the balloons together, one beneath the other, to form the shape of a winged angel. The room was dark, except for the glow of a small night-light, and in my confusion I had perceived the mass to be my guardian angel.

Slowly, my thoughts focused. Bypass surgery! The surgery that happens to someone else, but not to me. For three years the cardiologist had managed my heart blockages with medication. During that time I played the Pollyanna game fantasizing that somehow a new medical miracle would suddenly materialize, remove the blockages and correct my heart problems. But five days ago I was forced to face the truth. All of the available medications had been tried. Angioplasty would not work in my case. Bypass surgery was now my only alternative.

After the doctors had given this ultimatum I lay in silence thinking of the ordeal ahead. I had a history of allergies, severe side effects to medications and unusual reactions to anesthetics. What problems would this hypersensitivity cause? Too, I'd heard of others who experienced strokes after open heart surgery. Would that be my fate? If I should die, who would care for my aged mother? And what about my husband who depended on me? My mind and emotions overloaded with questions and doubts.

Then I recalled a formula to be used in times of crisis, a three-point plan presented thirty-five years ago by Mary Oler, a visiting speaker at a women's workshop. It was a fairly simple plan, but in the past I had not been able to keep all three steps in operation for any length of time. I decided to try the plan again.

One, DON'T PANIC. I seemed calm on the outside, but inwardly I wanted to flee the hospital, fly forty-five miles to our peaceful, quiet home in the country and never leave my comfortable surroundings.

That was foolish to contemplate for there was danger of a full-blown heart attack even while lying in my hospital bed. My responsibility was to relax and cooperate with the doctors and nurses.

Two, LOOK AROUND YOU AND HELP SOMEONE ELSE. Nine years ago my husband of thirty-four years had suffered two heart attacks. A year later my eighty-year-old mother endured a cardiac arrest. Both needed reassurance and a positive attitude about my surgery. Who better to give them that than I? For our two daughters and sons-in-law I could provide an example of faith and courage.

The three granddaughters were especially concerned about Nana. Elementary school children have not lived long enough to know from past experiences the promises of God. "And we know that in all things God works for the good of those who love him, who have been called according to his purpose." (Romans 8:28, NIV). With God's help my surgery could assist in building this belief into their lives.

There was another group to consider--my family of friends, a family not by birth but by choice. And as I gave to both of these families, I found myself receiving far more from them than I gave. Thinking of others and expressing those thoughts took my mind off myself and aided in the healing process.

Three, and the most important, RELY ON GOD. I Peter 5:7 says, "Cast all your anxiety on Him because He cares for you" (NIV). During my five decades of joy and sorrow, sickness and health, success and failure I had learned the importance of trusting in God. Many times I had decided to turn everything in my life over to Him, but each time I found myself grabbing back this and that as if to say, "Move over, God. I'll handle this myself."

But now, what else could I do but place myself in God's hands? This time, because of my helplessness, it was much easier to let go and let God have full control.

This period in my life was not easy for me or for my family. Recuperation was slow and frustrating with some complications. In the hospital, angels of mercy in the form of nurses, doctors, family and friends cared for me and comforted me. Later, at home, God continued to work through His servants, my friends, who ministered to me with calls, visits, cards and letters, by running errands and by furnishing nourishing meals prepared by caring hands.

Sometimes my chest-centered scar shows his ugly head above a lower-cut blouse or dress. I do not try to hide that man-made blemish on my skin; instead, I wear it with pride. Here is visible, positive evidence of what God, working through doctors, did to give me a second lease on life.

It is now two years since that dreaded bypass, and I am well and happy. I am not particularly aware I have a heart -- the way it is with persons who have normal, healthy organs. My mended heart is filled with faith, love and gratitude to God, my family and my friends.

I often think of the angel at my bedside. Perhaps at that low ebb in my life I needed reassurance -- yes, reassurance from a balloon angel -- that God was with me and would never fail me. (See Hebrews 13:5)

Geraldine Ketchum Crow is author of *Bloom Where you are Transplanted* (Life Press, 1996). She is a member of Chenal Valley Church of Christ, Little Rock, Arkansas

ETERNAL LOVE

Eve Braden Hatchett

Being an active senior citizen, healthy and somewhat happy, I was devastated when I could no longer walk except on a walker. I had met adversity head on--losing two husbands, an only child and beating cancer--I knew what scars the heart could take. I lived by "When God puts a period, don't put a question mark!"

Being a victim of silicone side effects, I fell and broke my ankle. After the break had healed, I began to lose my balance. I went from crutches, to a cane, to a four-prong cane, then to a walker. Next will be a wheelchair.

Friends help when they can. I have learned to move through the house at my own risk, knowing one slip and I'm on the floor. I can get the mail, feed the cats, fix a TV dinner, sponge bathe, dress myself and manage to fix my hair. The telephone with its long cord has almost been my downfall, but it is my only link to the outside.

I have learned from Romans that Paul said tribulations bring experience, experience brings patience and patience, hope. How true the Bible is.

There have been moments of despair, and the big "Why me?" But I have found that no matter what God had to do, I was still important to him. I was as much in his sight as the sparrow. He never lets me down. He always listens. Many tears have soaked my pillow on long, lonely nights, but he dried them with "Lo I am with you always...." (Matthew 28:20)

"Ask, and it shall be given you..." (Matthew 7:7) I repeat when I can't do a simple task and then a "Thank you, Jesus" after I tried and found He helped me. I know I wade in deep waters, but God won't let it overflow. He has more

59

of my attention now; for when I am weakest, I'm strongest through him. I have more time to read his word and learn about the victory in store for all of us who believe.

I once had to go to the doctor in a cab and I thought, "There's no one to be with me." Then I almost heard "I'll be with you," and Jesus and I went bravely on, unafraid.

"Sick and ye visited me not, hungry and ye fed me not." (Matthew 25:42) These words ring in my heart. When God gives me back my ability to walk and drive, my feet will take me to the shut-ins. I can read to them, be their feet, cheer them up and let them know how to love one another. It is the inner man God sees--not his imperfect body. "My flesh and my heart faileth, but God is the strength of my heart, and my portion for ever." (Psalms 73:26)

Eve Braden Hatchett is author of *Take Time to Laugh* and *Of Butterflies and Unicorns* and is a member of Highland Street Church of Christ, Memphis, Tennessee.

A SUDDEN EXPERIENCE WITH GRIEF

Cynthia Moore

The Advent Season of 1979 was an especially beautiful one for our family. Our daughter was a senior in high school and thinking of college, and our church was experiencing growth in numbers and spirit. On the Monday following the Chancel Choir's presentation of Handel's *Messiah,* we were feeling the power of joy and love that is such a vital part of this wonderful season.

Suddenly without warning, we received word that my husband's mother had been killed that morning in an automobile accident. What made it even more difficult was that his father had been killed in a similar accident 29 years earlier.

We were devastated! My mother-in-law was only 63 and had been in good health. We were overcome with emotion and dreaded the duty of telling our daughter about the death of her grandmother, whom she loved dearly. Our son, who was home from college, was at home when the call came in.

Bob and I had our cry together and then cried with our daughter when she came home for lunch. We began making arrangements with Bob's brother and sister and their families to come to Memphis and have the funeral services here. We could not wait to get together to share in our grief together. Our love for one another and for my mother-in-law was a strengthening factor in our sudden grief. We were all people of faith and had the assurance that God was with us and that my mother-in-law was with Him.

Our colleagues in the ministry and the members of our congregation surrounded us with their love and care for us. We had ministered to them in their times of trouble, and now they ministered to us.

In our moment of sudden grief, it was being a part of a loving family and a caring church that gave us the courage, strength, and power to move through this traumatic time in our lives.

Cynthia Moore participates in all activities at Bartlett United Methodist Church, Bartlett, Tennessee, where her husband is Senior Pastor. Her life centers around her husband, her family and her church.

I BELIEVE

"The Lord will guide you always; he will satisfy your needs in a sun-scorched land and will strengthen your frame. You will be like a well-watered garden, like a spring where waters never fail." Isaiah 58:11 (NIV)

"I can do everything through him who gives me strength." Philippians 4:13 (NIV)

As a farmer's wife I know what it like to need rain and to feel joy when it comes. As a women with a large family, I have shared with my loved ones many kinds of pain.

As I get older it seems disappointments such as losses become increasingly more common. Instead of dwelling on the loss, I try to remember my loved ones in a loving way and be thankful for the time I had with them. Sometimes I have to put my personal grief aside in order to comfort the living.

Jesus knows all our sorrows as well as joy. It was for our tears he died. He is closer than we think. Jesus said he would not leave us alone or comfortless. That He would always be with us in our deepest sorrow or on the mountain top.

Dorothy Bullard Tacker

The mother of six children one of which is editor Frances Cowden, Dorothy Tacker sings in the choir at Joiner United Methodist Church, Joiner, Arkansas.

ON THE DEATH OF MY PARENTS

Elaine Nunnally Davis

Just before waking early in the morning of Friday, March 21, 1980, I had a dream about my mother. I was going through troubled times in my career and I had been very happy that my mother and I had finally developed the good relationship we had never had as I was growing up. We hadn't rehashed the past; we had just dropped it and begun again with the present.

She had felt my distress the Sunday before when my granddaughter and I had taken her a present for her birthday on Wednesday. About dark she had called long distance to ask if there were anything she could do to help me. I had a feeling that there was something on Mother's mind that she hadn't said to me during the year preceding her death. Though I knew what it was, I never pressed her for it. Even with the call, she didn't mention it.

Mother's childhood had been troubled and her marriage had been no better. Mother remembered the house full of arguments and full of children and bottles and wet diapers for ten children. Perhaps she had seen her marriage as a way to escape from all that. The man she married, however, wanted "a dozen children around his dinner table." Mother suddenly saw herself tied down at home with Daddy off enjoying himself. It was a tumultuous nine years that they lived together, pulling one against the other.

I can imagine their disappointment when I was born, the third child and the third girl. Less than two years later, I was followed by a boy. There was never any room in the family for me. My oldest sister was mother's helper; the next girl became mother's helper's assistant, and my brother was the baby and the boy.

Mother pulled my oldest sister into her battle with Daddy and she was accompanied by her assistant in the antagonism. I loved Daddy. I wasn't ever mad at Daddy. He was the only one who ever gave me any attention. It was through him that God taught me what love felt like. When Daddy left just before my fifth birthday, I lost my support. All the "sins" of Daddy were heaped on "Daddy's girl." I became the scapegoat.

Once when there had been a tremendous tirade against the absent husband and father, I took a pencil and wrote on the bottom of his picture, "I love you anyway." I was soundly trounced for it. Never again did I resist my three older tormentors. I did, however, spend a tremendous amount of time and energy maintaining my own personal integrity in my heart. In short, I grew up alone in enemy territory.

Except for the absence of a father we appeared to be a model family. Mother took care of us and she was praised. When she vented her frustration on us with vicious tongue-lashings, it was always behind closed doors. And she really was frustrated. She had four children to raise and little or no income on which to do it. She had no help in decision making. She had no one to relieve her when she was exhausted.

I never felt my mother was mean. I recognized, somehow, her frustration, though I cannot say when that fact first occurred to me. Once we had grown up, Mother got medical attention and was relieved of that problem. Financially, things were better. Mother began going to another church near her home and singing alto in a quartet there. She began to study the word of God. She finally began to understand love and to share that love with me.

The reactions of my sisters and me was quite different when Mother died. My oldest sister expressed her anger that mother had finally come to a place in life where things were not so difficult and then she had died. I was thrilled for mother's sake that she was with God and totally relieved of all pain and distress. I couldn't imagine why anyone could want to stay here rather than to be in heaven.

In my personal life, I was devastated. I had intended to ask Mother in June whether I might return home to live with her because I was so alone. That summer I was at the lowest point in my whole life. In my loneliness, I took a weekend job. It was almost a year later, in April, that I first met the husband God had prepared for me. He became my new boss at that time. A year later we were married.

The following spring I saw a Jimmy Stewart movie on television and for some reason it reminded me of my father. I began to have concerns about his dying and made a vow to go visit him monthly. The last time I saw him, he said he had something he wanted me to have. It was a negative. I took it home, looked at it, couldn't quite make out what it was, and laid it on the bookshelf. In September he died.

The next year was really difficult for me. I came home from work every day, crying for my father and my mother. I cried every time I saw a father and a daughter on television. My grief for my mother returned in full force as I realized that I was cut completely loose from my family. My husband was wonderful and worried. It was during this time in late November and early December of 1983 that I wrote a poem about my grief:

> Death dealt to me a double blow
> And laid my trembling spirit low.
> While still the first I did deny,
> Immediately, a second lie.
>
> Reverberations fill my soul:
> Does death not come but to the old?
> The villain spirit pressed his case
> And did his work too fast apace.
>
> He first took her who gave me life,

Who'd made her peace and ended strife,
And three years thence he came once more
And claimed a dad whom I adore.

My spirit, rootless, too alone,
Can scarce be raised from posture prone.
Not whole, each day I seek for peace
And pray that time will bring surcease.

When I received the call about nine on Friday morning that Mother had died earlier, I knew that my dream had not really been a dream at all. My mother had paid me a final visit in the spirit to say the thing she had wanted to say.

The negative Daddy gave me was the last family picture of all of us, taken forty years earlier. It was a picture that I had never seen.

My grief goes beyond the simple death of my parents, though that fact is difficult enough. With their deaths within three years, my family of origin disintegrated. My consolation lies in the teaching of Jesus about the family of God. "And he looked round about on them which sat about him, and said, "Behold my mother and my brethren! For whoever shall do the will of God, the same is my brother, and my sister, and mother (Mark 3:34-35). God will restore the years the locusts have eaten.

Elaine Nunnally Davis is a member of Christ United Methodist Church, Memphis, Tennessee and is author of Life Press publications, *The Mothers of Jesus* (1994) and *Eve's Fruit* (1995).

HOLDING MY HAND

Aline Thompson

Some years ago, when I was going through a divorce, it was a difficult time of much pain and adjustment. I was experiencing so much anxiety that I wonder today how I was even able to function. There were days when I was so overcome with worry about "what ifs" and "the worst that could possibly happen" that I couldn't eat, and would dread the weekends if I had time that wasn't filled with activities or people. I even came down with a case of pneumonia when I had to be separated from my precious two-year-old son David (for whom I desperately tried to hold onto my sanity).

During that time I read a book by Norman Vincent Peale that had the verse from 1 Peter 5:7, "Cast all your anxieties on Him, for He cares for you." (NIV)

That means he cares for Aline! This verse had made such an impression that I cross-stitched the words, had it framed, and it is in my office to this day.

I wish I could remember how this next, very significant thing occurred, but I can't. I don't know if the Holy Spirit put it in my mind or if one of my many supportive Christian friends or family members shared this with me. Whenever I was overwhelmed with fear and anxiety, instead of focusing on the fear itself, I pictured Jesus holding my hand, walking beside me every step of the way. And I repeated to myself "Jesus is holding my hand, Jesus is holding my hand." And with Jesus holding my hand, I can make it through anything. "Yes, Lord, I can feel your hand in mine right now."

"Do not be anxious about anything, but in everything, by prayer and petition, with thanksgiving, let your requests be known to God. And the peace of God that transcends all understanding will guard your hearts and your minds in Christ Jesus." Philippians 4:6-7 (NIV).

Thank you, Lord for caring so much, even about the details of our lives. Help us to keep our eyes on the sweet face of Jesus and not on our troubles. All praise and glory belong to you. Amen.

Aline Thompson is Clinical Lead RN, Methodist Hospice and a member of Colonial Park United Methodist Church, Memphis, Tennessee.

"JESUS WEPT!"

Gladys Ellis

Frank was only forty-nine years old when he was told he had cancer of the vocal cords. He would have to have a laryngectomy, removal of his vocal cords. His surgery lasted all of a long November day. After twelve hours the surgeon reported that not all of the cancer could be removed, and the cancer would come back. I felt that day that I had already lost the one closest to me in all the world. That December it seemed to me unfair that the city was filled with happy Christmas shoppers and carols were ringing in shopping malls and from TV and radio, while I was grieving and alone. But, of course, I was not alone-- God answered my prayer for strength for Frank and for me.

In the months that followed, Frank underwent surgery six more times. Even though we were told after each operation that the cancer had spread beyond the reach of the surgeon's knife, we felt comforted and sustained. I knew during those dark days that God cared for us and grieved for us in our sorrow. I wasn't aware at that time, however, of the full meaning of the words "Jesus wept." John 11:35.

I know now that He was not weeping just for the sadness in the hearts of Mary and Martha as they mourned the death of their brother Lazarus. Jesus was weeping for all the sorrows that would come to all of his children through the ages. Knowing that we have a Savior who always feels our sorrows and reaches out to comfort us is surely the greatest of blessings.

Frank is one of the fortunate ones who was eventually cured by an experimental treatment at M. C. Anderson Research and Tumor Clinic in Houston, Texas.

We give thanks for every day of the twenty additional years he has been given, and we will always remember that Jesus wept for us.

Gladys Ellis is a retired English teacher from Memphis City Schools. She now teaches for the Memphis Literacy Council. She is a part of the prayer ministry and an Adult Sunday School teacher at Colonial Park United Methodist Church, Memphis, Tennessee.

The Lord bless you and keep you; the Lord make His face to shine upon you and be gracious to you. The Lord turn His face toward you and give you peace. Numbers 6:24-26 (NIV)

TRUSTING

Blanche Boren

We were taught to believe this message from God's word. I grew up in south Georgia. When I was five my mother died, and my sister and I went to live with my father's parents. My grandparents were kind and loving. They taught us to love and trust the Lord. Because He was with us, we would never be alone.

When I was twelve, my dear grandmother died. This was another sad time for us. I tried hard to remember what she taught us--Jesus would always be with us and give us peace if we only believed.

At this time my father became my everything. He was a kind, loving and caring father. He was always there for my sister Nell and me. Many times I could tell it was hard for him.

When I fell in love with my precious husband, there was one problem. He lived in Memphis, Tennessee, which was seven hundred fifty miles from my home in Savannah, Georgia. It was a time of being torn by my wanting to make a life with my husband whom I loved and being so far away from my father who needed me.

My visits to Savannah were quite often during the first few years of my marriage, though my sister Nell was still at home. When she married and left my father alone, it was even more of a worry for me. I wanted to be there for him as he had been there for me. I prayed a lot and God did help me find peace.

72

God blessed my husband and me with two wonderful children, Richard and Kathy. My life was a joy caring for my precious children and my huband. However, I still worried about my father who was so far away and alone.

When my father was in his early sixties, he met my stepmother, who was a widow. She is a good person who loved and cared for my father twenty-six years. I felt better about him. I still worried, however, that he would be sick or die and I wouldn't be with him.

I remembered what my grandmother taught me: Trust God and He will give you peace. I prayed many times for God to work it out for me to be with my father at the end.

Time passed. My children grew up and had children of their own.

One day in September, my husband told me he was holding a sales seminar in Atlanta beginning February 27 and suggested I take a week off and go with him. He suggested that Nell and I visit my father. That was the plan until February 25 when my stepmother called and told us that my father was going in the hospital for a test on the 26th.

Later when I called his room, a nurse told me he was having a heart attack and they were moving him to the ICU.

I then called my sister in Atlanta and my husband who was in Nashville and made arrangements to fly to Atlanta. I would meet Nell there and we would go on to Savannah.

I called the airport and the next flight to Atlanta was in one hour and fifteen minutes. I live twenty-five minutes from the airport. I asked them to book me, thinking all the time how am I going to make the flight on time?

A friend came over and called my sister and gave her my arrival time, went to the bank, and helped me pack. Believe it or not, with the help of Christian friends, we made it.

At the airport I ran into Kim, a longtime Christian friend who is blind but travels a lot. Sometime in the past I had shared my fears of flying with her and of not being with my father at the end. She said, "I'll pray for you to have peace on your flight and that you and your sister will get to Savannah to be with your father before it's too late." My God gave me a great peace that day.

My flight was thirty minutes late leaving Memphis but arrived in Atlanta three minutes early. I was on time and had peace.

My sister and I stayed at the hospital ICU waiting room with my stepmother from Thursday until Sunday night. Sunday many of my parent's church friends came by to visit us. By late afternoon we had not found time to eat. When my sister and stepmother went out to get something to eat, I picked up a pamphlet, *Daily Word.* When I opened it, there were these words, "Moving Day is Coming."

The article was about a minister who was dying with cancer, but contained words of peace to the family he was leaving behind. God put this in my hand to read at this time; for, you see, my father's moving day was to be that day.

A few minutes later my cousin, who is a minister, came in with his wife. He asked if he might go in to see my father. Father had his eyes closed and my cousin thought he was asleep. When I touched his hand, he opened his eyes and spoke. When my cousin asked how he was, he answered, "Just fine. I'm at peace."

My cousin said a prayer. Father thanked him and then asked me to take my stepmother home to get some rest. I promised to do that soon.

My stepmother went in to say goodnight and we left for her home, which was less than five minutes from the hospital. My cousin and his wife decided to go with us for a cup of coffee and a short visit, since we live far away from each other. I was in the kitchen making coffee when my husband called from Atlanta. The nurse broke in on the line and asked us to come back to the hospital. When we arrived there, my father had gone to be with his Savior in his heavenly home.

My cousin, being a minister, took charge of gathering his personal things and had a prayer with us. He then went home with us and made all the necessary arrangements.

Numbers 6:26 says, "The Lord turn His face toward you and give you peace." (NIV) Believe me, He gave me this peace that passes all earthly understanding.

I'll never forget how my God planned all this out for me. You see, God had planned this months ahead when in September my husband asked me to take time off to make a trip with him.

Blanche Boren serves in the prayer ministry and is active in the United Methodist Women at Colonial Park United Methodist Church, Memphis, Tennessee.

TO LOVE AND TO CHERISH

Frances Darby

In less than a month Jim and I will be celebrating our 49th wedding anniversary. What are our plans? To live and appreciate each moment we are allowed to share. I speak of moments because advance planning must be very flexible in the life of a patient whose body and mind are locked in the rigidity of Parkinsonism. The balance in life weighs heavily toward a possible infection, a lapse of memory as to who he thinks I am or even if he knows me at all. If I suffer under such alleged attacks I must remember that he, too, is suffering.

I cannot know what is going on in his mind, so I content myself into believing he knows. It has been hard for a very active sports fan with a brilliant mind to accept a totally dependent life spent in a stroke chair all day.

We will begin the day with Jim being fed breakfast in bed at which time I will remind him of the importance of the day. I will search his electric blue eyes to possibly find a twinkle of recognition before the far-away stare returns. It is moments of lucidity such as this to which I cling. Often times even in their brevity of time, I gain strength and courage to face the day.

The Nurses Aide arrives at 8 a.m. in the morning to bathe, dress and move him with the Hoyer lift from the bed to the stroke chair. This is a most tiring ordeal for him, and he usually spends the morning dozing or watching the birds from the window of the sun room. Each day brings surprises, pain, heartaches and yes, even joy.

Jim's appetite is very good, which makes it pleasurable to cook for him. He will try to feed himself. The Aide leaves at four o'clock. The strain of the day will be on his face; my strength also is waning, and my body cries for rest. Soon our quiet supper is over and I move him from the chair to the bed. Quality time each night to express thanksgiving and gratitude for life and shared moments together gives us both the calm to move into continued hope in the future.

10/16/93

PARKINSON'S -- THIRD STAGE

Life is staring me in the face
Baring the tendency to turn my head
In an attempt to avoid
The lonely, empty hurting
that lingers
In the knowledge
that you are leaving me -

Your illness has stripped you
of all dignity
Mobility and even for the most part
cognizance

Tenderness that we share
from you is seen
when your heavenly blue eyes
reflect appreciation
or a clinging grasp of the hand
after I have given you a rub down
a hug and even lifted a song or prayer

You sleep peacefully

My desire to care for your every need
Far outweighs my physical strength

Emotions drained or deadened
Draw heavily on the spirit
Banishing all but faith and hope

For the moment I am fulfilled
In the knowledge that renewed strength
Comes from the true source
God.

Frances Darby is active in a MIFA Caregivers Support Group and is a member of a writing group at East Center, Gaisman, Memphis, Tennessee.

IN CHRISTIAN FELLOWSHIP

MORE THAN CAKE AND COFFEE

She held my hand when darkness
    seemed too near;
As death clouds hovered over us we cried
And went into the prayer room with our fear
To seek His loving presence by our side . . .
        moonlight tears
        noontime laughter . . .
        we were
        together!
On picnic grounds or in intensive care
We shared our chocolate cake or ice cream bars
I listened to her real-life soaps and there
She held my hand when darkness hid the stars.

FBC

79

If you have any encouragement from being united with Christ, if any comfort from his love, if any fellowship with the Spirit, if any tenderness and compassion, then make my joy complete by being like-minded, having the same love, being one in spirit and purpose....Each of you should look not only to your own interests, but also to the interests of others. Philippians 2:1-2, 4 (NIV)

Therefore, since we are surrounded by such a great cloud of witnesses, let us throw off everything that hinders and the sin that so easily entangles, and let us run with perseverance the race marked out for us. Let us fix our eyes on Jesus, the author and perfecter of our faith, who for the joy set before him endured the cross, scorning its shame, and sat down at the right hand of the throne of God.

Hebrews 12:1-2 (NIV)

SURROUNDED BY A CLOUD OF WITNESSES

Reverend Bob Moore

Memorial day is a time to honor and remember those who have died for our country. It is also a sacred time in our church to honor the memory of our loved ones who are now a part of the church triumphant. We pay tribute to those members of our congregation who have recently departed the physical life to enter God's eternity. But we also remember in our hearts all our loved ones from whom we have been separated by death. Each of us has special memories of these special people in our lives. There are few, if any, who have not walked in the valley of grief and sorrow due to the death of a close loved one. We commemorate all our loved ones who have gone beyond our sight, and to God we say our thanks for the hope of seeing them again.

"Wherefore, we are surrounded by so great a cloud of witnesses." The writer of the book of Hebrews was referring to the heroes of faith, many of whom he had named in the eleventh chapter, but also the many faithful who are known only to God and to those special to them. As we live and worship, this cloud of witnesses surrounds us with challenge, comfort, and encouragement. Let me suggest some things they might have to say to us today.

Death is real and unavoidable.

Our cloud of witnesses would testify that death is real and for all of us it is unavoidable. Death is something that comes to everything in the universe; it is a part of the natural cycle of life. Those of you who have recently given up a loved one know well the reality of death with its separation, grief, loneliness and adjustment.

In our society we have always tried in every way to take death lightly, to disguise its presence, to live and act as if it was not a reality we must all face. One of the early heresies of the church was that of "Docetism." It was an attempt to say that Jesus did not really die; he only seemed to. But the creeds of the church reject this kind of thinking and make clear and bluntly so, that Jesus was crucified, dead, and buried. Even to Jesus death was real.

Death is not the end, it is another beginning.

But our cloud of witnesses would not linger long on this note, but would move quickly to assure us that death is not the end; it is another beginning. Death with all its realism is not the finale of a person's life. The cloud of witnesses speaking out of their experience would witness to the continuation of the self in a new and better world.

Almost everyone who has died and has been resuscitated is no longer afraid of dying. Such people have experienced a preview of the after life and now look forward to it.

In Jesus's experience with the cross and the tomb, we witness the power of resurrection, a power released in our world and available to all who believe. The gospel proclaims that even though it is our nature to die, God through Christ resurrects us to a new and eternal life.

The cloud of witnesses would say to us: "Mourn for your loss and broken relationship, but mourn not for us, we have been resurrected and are new creatures in God!" They would echo and remind us of the words of John's gospel: "For God so loved the world that he gave his only son, that whosoever believeth in him shall not perish, but have everlasting life." John 3:16.

Death and grief can be sensitizing and strengthening.

The cloud of witness might also remind us that our experience with death and grief can sensitize us to others in their need and strengthen us to be a help to others.

I read one interpreter who wrote that the second of Jesus' great beatitudes could also be translated: "Blessed are those who mourn, for they shall become comforters." Because of our experience with death and sorrow, we are made capable of understanding and empathizing with the grieving of others.

Henri Nouwen wrote a book about this several years ago and coined a phrase that speaks powerfully. He called us "wounded healers." Sometimes it is our scars that make persons open to us and our help. This is the power that many have experienced in grief recovery groups. Being with others who are walking the same path and feeling the same hurt allow us to help one another.

This is part of the power and meaning of the incarnation: God's entrance and involvement in the totality of our life. Because God in Christ has experienced our troubles, our sorrows, our adversities, and even our death, God understands and his presence is our comfort and hope.

I believe that God does draw nearer to us in these moments of intense need and in his power and presence we are enabled to do what we thought was impossible.

The cloud of witnesses encircles us and encourages us.

The writer of Hebrews envisioned not only God's help, but saw the cloud of witnesses encircling us and encouraging us to keep on keeping on.

The cloud of witnesses surrounds us to strengthen us in our journey through the valley of the shadow of death, but also to call us to remember who we are and to whom we ever belong.

A young 19-year-old man was leading a memorial service for his and his family's beloved grandfather. As a part of that service, he had all the children and grandchildren to stand. He then said to them: "Granddaddy is in everyone of you--don't do anything to reflect badly on that name!"

The cloud of witnesses reminds us that those we love are a part of us and that we also are created in the very image of God himself, and challenges us to do nothing that would reflect badly on the images within us.

The writer of Hebrews with his vision of being surrounded by a cloud of witnesses envisions our life as a race and calls us to move on with life, running and living with perseverance and looking unto Jesus as our focus and motivation. As we remember those we love and those who have gone before us, let us listen for their word to us today. We might hear them say: "Keep the faith and the faith will keep you!"

Excerpts from a sermon given while Senior Pastor at Colonial Park United Methodist Church, Memphis, Tennessee. Bob Moore is now Senior Pastor of Bartlett United Methodist Church, Bartlett, Tennessee.

TEPPI

Christine Lundwall

Out of a torturous past there came a man and his daughter. They became my next door neighbors.

In the world out here, away from Sunday School, my concept of a "good neighbor" had changed considerably. Because of past next door neighbors (on both sides of me), who had drunk, doped, fought, played their stereos so loud I couldn't enjoy the quiet within my own home, and with their children vandalizing my property, I was in no mood to be neighborly. My position was: "I'll leave you alone, and you leave me alone."

In just a few days after moving in, this little slip of a girl happened to be outside where I was, childlike as most children no longer are, introduced herself, "Hello, my name is Teppi." I responded, friendly enough on the outside, but aloof on the inside--and so I remained for the next year or so.

The man kept his back yard neat and mowed, and I worked in mine; but I took care that I didn't get involved in any over-the-backyard-fence conversations.

As time went on, I realized he worked until 10 p.m., leaving his young daughter alone--and I began to worry about her. Even though I was a seasoned veteran at worrying about others' problems that I could do nothing about, I drew a circle around myself and my "space." I told myself I could not mother all the children in this world, even Teppi.

She (and the two tikes on the other side of me) never pushed themselves on me; so gradually I began to mellow a little. There was a little cake baking now and then and some cookie making along the way.

And then the man was struck with lung cancer. At

first, there was an occasional loaf of freshly baked bread or a little transportation--to and from school when he was unable to drive.

As my concept of a good neighbor changed once again, we even began talking about such things as the Power of a Real God.

A little over three weeks ago my neighbor James had to decide whether to go to a Hospice for the brief time left to him and put his daughter in a foster home. She had been doing all the housekeeping and care giving, going with him on the emergency midnight rides to the hospital, caring for the dog and cats, all the laundry--and attending school at the same time--a slip of a 17-year-old girl.

Proper nutrition was his problem, James said. So I began cooking for them as I cooked for myself. Just two weeks ago--it seems like years--I'll always remember James enthusiastically polishing off two platefuls of fresh peas, creamed corn, fried okra, sliced tomatoes, and cornbread--saving the apple pie for later. A bare short week later, he made his last midnight trip to the hospital and left this existence at 10:00 o'clock the next morning, Teppi at his side.

After a short visit with a Sunday School teacher and another short visit with my daughter in the country near Kentucky Lake, Teppi stayed with me until the Department of Human Services could make proper arrangements for her to be with her own family, a half sister and her husband.

The other family members were unable to come even to claim his body. But somehow, I sensed a funeral was a critical need for Teppi. The following Wednesday, someone from Smith's Funeral Home called us to invite us to a grave side service for James; Teppi came to life!

An hour or so later the social worker from the Department of Human Services called with the sensational news that the necessary investigation of Teppi's family was completed; and she would be flying to Pennsylvania on Saturday to begin a new life.

There was a notice of her father's death in the

obituary section of the *Jackson Sun*. The short clipping and a snapshot of Teppi and her father were properly glued into the Bible given to her by the Highland Park Baptist Church in memory of her father. It seemed to me to be critical for Teppi to know her father's existence and passing had been noticed by his fellow men.

There were about fifteen to twenty people at Highland Memorial Gardens that Thursday morning. Teppi's Pastor, Jerry Eggenberger, delivered a beautifully simple message from Psalms. He closed with a heartfelt prayer for her and then asked her if she wanted to say something.

Teppi stood and told how much she had loved her Dad, how he had cared for her through all the hard times, and what he had taught her, what she wanted to do with her life (to teach and take care of little children). I felt I was living a drama that few are privileged to experience. We were all crying. I shall never forget Teppi at that service; each time I look at the picture of that simple little bouquet she bought at Big Lots, the only flowers decorating James's casket, I'll remember her and how she cried, sobbing, in the arm of another loving neighbor.

We then left James, drove home and began the rest of her life with a Going Away Party at Magic Wheels. Friends and teachers from her Special Education Class, and the Hospice social worker were there--15 of us in all.

To augment a cake Teppi had made the night before, Magic Wheels provided a private room, ice cream, cokes and decorations. There were gifts, lots of hugs and pictures--and skating.

Friday was a big day tying up all the loose ends at doctors' offices, etc. At 7 p.m., both of us tired, we took one more shopping trip to the Mall, to buy something special for the plane trip.

Teppi is a shopper in her own right. With absolutely no advice and guidance from me, she decided against the more expensive garments at the Mall and suggested we go to tried-and-true Wal-Mart. It was there she found a flowery frock that transformed little Teppi, in her usual shorts and bra tops, into a young lady, walking on *Cloud Nine* in her own "Alice Blue Gown."

Home at 9:30, she ate half of a Burger King Special, took a bath and then The Dress! Gone was the fatigue. Gone was the need for sleep. Her brother-in-law called and they talked for some time and Teppi giggled! The first time I'd ever heard her giggle!

I took my weary body to bed, but got up a while later. Seeing her light on and the door ajar, I knocked and poked my head in. I saw she had moved a full length mirror, stored behind the door, to front and center, where she could see herself and the dress.

"When you want to go to bed, wake me, I'll unzip the back," I told her and went back to bed and sleep.

I wasn't surprised the next morning to find her sound asleep, most comfortable in The Dress!

At 6:30 a.m. she was busily applying her makeup (she seldom wears any at all). At 6:45 she asked me, "Is my makeup all right!" Again, I was amazed--just enough rouge for a soft blush and just enough lipstick. She was "made up" to look as if she didn't have any on--altogether a professional job!

At 10 o'clock sharp, her ride was here. Pictures of her had been taken, her bags were loaded. She was a luscious-looking "piece of cake" dressed in blue, happily waving good-bye to us, bound for a new home and a new life.

With a drained, empty fatigue, I know I'll miss her. But I know this past week has been a gift from God, showing me there are all kinds of people who care, and in caring for Teppi's needs at this time, I somehow cared for my own.

Christine Lundwall is a member of West Jackson Baptist Church and is active in community service in Jackson, Tennessee.

When I consider the heavens, the work of thy fingers;
the moon and stars, which thou has ordained; what is man that
thou art mindful of him?...For thou hast made him a little
lower than the angels and hast crowned him with glory and
honor. Psalms 8:3-5

LIVING WITH OUR GRIEF

Laura Hartmann

Recently, I attended the funeral of a man whom I had not seen in years. I had such fond memories of the way in which he touched my life long ago. I, like so many others, felt the need to attend his funeral--a service of worship to the dedication of his life to God.

Among responsibilities, he was the choir director of his church. And that's how I remember him. He was one of those people that showed me God's love through music, through life, and through love.

Over the many years, my love for music has grown. From the little girl who would attend choir rehearsals in awe with her mother; to now, the adult mother who still attends choir rehearsals (in another sister church and under another director) in awe. For, it truly can be a spiritual experience.

At this man's funeral, his choir sang "The Majesty and Glory of Your Name" by Linda Lee Johnson and Tom Fettke. It is a beautiful anthem of faith based on Psalm 8.

Listening to the choir sing so beautifully, and loving this anthem, which I too have sung, I felt so much that day. So many emotions were awakened by this music. When we are faced with a death, we experience separation, sorrow, and loss.

We are separated from the one we love. We cannot go back and say what we wish we had said or do what we had meant to do. And this brings sorrow to us. We feel a loss that we will never again be able to be with this person who has died.

But that is how music for me becomes a comfort. It taps into our emotions and sparks memories from our lives and how we interacted on the earth. It awakens joy to know that someone we love has accomplished this earthly life and has gone ahead to take on an eternal body and reside in peace with God.

I just finished reading Barbara Bush's book, *A Memoir,* in which she dedicated the book to faith, family, and friends. She also ended the book by speaking of how these are the things that really matter in life. How I agree!

Through our faith, we find hope and peace when we face death. Through family and friends, we find comfort. And that is what this beautiful anthem says to me, that the majesty and glory of God's name is to be praised. God is mindful of man, His creation; God will bring us with love through those tough times of separation, sorrow, and loss. God will sustain us through our faith by our family and friends. "Alleluia, Alleluia, ALLELUIA!"

Laura Hartmann is active in the Chancel Choir, Colonial Park United Methodist Church and works as a Physical Therapist, at Methodist Hospital, Memphis, TN

WEEDS IN THE FIELD OF LIFE

Reverend Bob Moore

We have been trying to explain the presence of evil and suffering in the world since time began. In fact, volumes have been written by some of the smartest philosophers and by the greatest theologians. Yet with all these answers, we still struggle deep within our hearts with the question.

When we turn to the Bible for its answer, we discover it is almost silent on the subject. Some scholars say that Job is the only biblical book that focuses on the problem of evil, recognizing that the good also suffer and calling in to question the belief that all suffering is the result of sin, and yet with all its depth of struggle with the issue, it concludes that human suffering is a mystery.

There are no easy, simple answers from the human perspective to this perplexing issue. For as Paul wrote in his great essay on love in I Corinthians: "We see in a mirror dimly or distortedly...now we know in part."

There are no answers, but the parable in the thirteenth chapter of Matthew gives some insights into life and destiny, and on God's activity in our midst. There are a multiplicity of ideas and meanings in the obscure but powerful parable.

Another parable he put before them, saying, "The kingdom of heaven is likened unto a man which sowed good seed in his field; but while men slept, his enemy came and sowed tares among the wheat, and went his way. But when the blade was sprung up and brought forth fruit, then appeared the tares also. And the servants of the householder came and said unto him,

*'Sir, didst not thou sow good seed in thy field? From
whence then hath it tares?'*

*He said unto them, 'An enemy hath done this.'
The servants said unto him, 'Wilt thou then that we go
and gather them up?'*

*But he said. 'No; lest while ye gather up the
tares, ye root up also the wheat with them.'*

*Let both grow together until the harvest; and
in the time of harvest I will say to the reapers,
'Gather ye together first the tares, and bind them
in bundles to burn them: but gather the
wheat into my barn.'"* Matthew 13: 24-30

There are weeds in the field of life. There
always has been and there always will be. It is a part of
the human condition and the result of the gift of
freedom.

As much as we would like it not to be, life has its
troubles and difficulties. In Jesus' parable of the
foundations, the storms of life beat on the house founded
on the rock as well as the house founded on the sand.
There is no escape from trouble and sorrow; it is a part of
the human dilemma and none of us is exempt.

The parable also reminds us that some things can
not be changed, they have to be accepted, lived with and
lived through, at least for the time being. There are
weeds in the fields of life. There always have been and
always will be. We must learn to live through some of
the weeds that invade the fields of our lives.

God is not responsible for the weeds. Jesus'
word for us concerning the presence of evil, trouble, and
sorrow represented by the weeds is to assure us that God
is not responsible for the weeds. To the question, "Why
are there weeds in the field?" Jesus' answer in the parable
is, "An enemy has done this." The master sowed only
good seeds. The creation is good. It is not God's
intention that bad things should happen to any of us. It
is God's intention that the field should be perfect. The

Master has sowed only good seeds, but something or someone has sowed weeds and distorted the good creation, whether it be the forces of nature, the power and principalities of the world, evil within others or even ourselves. Jesus says, "An enemy has done this."

In a world filled with trouble and tribulation, we need to know and believe that God has not sent these difficulties and life storms upon us, but stands with us and suffers with us in these trying and difficult times. As God was with Christ through the agony of the cross, so God is with us in the agonies of our life. God did not promise us a rose garden, but he did promise to be with us. The great promise of the scriptures from beginning to the end is, "I will be with you."

Isaiah 41:10 is reflected in the words from the hymn, "How Firm a Foundation."

Fear not, I am with thee, O' be not dismayed
for I am thy God and will still give thee aid;
I'll strengthen and help thee, and cause thee to
stand
upheld by my righteous, omnipotent hand.

Dr. Leonard Sweet, who is President of the United Theological Seminary, tells about a woman who was a member of a church he served some years ago. Her name was Wilma. Dr. Sweet said she had the worst attitude he had ever encountered...always sullen, somber, cynical, sour, bitter, pessimistic. She was angry with life, against everything and critical of everyone. He wondered why. He looked into it and discovered that she had not always been this way. To the contrary, just a few years before, she had been quite the opposite: bright, happy, positive, energetic, and optimistic.

He found out that five years earlier, a drunk driver had run his car up on the sidewalk and hit Wilma's two year-old daughter, Kristi, killing her instantly. Wilma was devastated. Someone who had attempted to comfort her during her time of grief said a terrible thing to Wilma trying to explain Kristi's death. Someone had said, "Wilma, every now and then God gets tired of stale, worn-out flowers, and he wants a fresh young rosebud for his bouquet."

Dr. Sweet said when he heard that, he understood why Wilma was so bitter. He could not wait to get to her and say to her, "Wilma, don't you believe that for another minute. It was not God's will for your two-year old daughter to die. It was not God's will that Kristi should be hit by a car. It happened because a man made a bad decision. He tried to drive while he was drunk. That's what did it, not God. God's heart was broken too."

God did not put the weeds in the field, but they are there nevertheless. I wish there were no suffering, no slaughter of the innocent, no Somalia, no Bosnia, no Rwanda, no accidents, no violence in our cities, no abuse of children or spouses, no weeds in the field. But without the possibility of evil, there can be no good. Without the possibility of not loving, there can be no love, without the possibility of not believing there can be no faith. Without God limiting his control of us and our circumstances, there can be no freedom and real life. God does not cause the weeds but his gift of freedom for human beings allows their presence. There are weeds in the field, but God is not responsible for them.

Yes, we are destined to live in a world with weeds, and these weeds often bring pain and sorrow. God is not the cause of the weeds, but he is with us. In the midst of it all, God calls us to be the wheat and empowers us by grace to do it. As wheat we shall be measured by how much we have loved: how we loved God and our neighbor and how we expressed that love in the deeds of our life, in our caring concern, our gestures of kindness and encouragement, our binding of wounds, in the pain we eased, in the loneliness we dispelled, in the burdens we lightened.

Dr. Sweet's illustration was used with permission.

CELEBRATION

Let not your heart be troubled ye believe in God, believe also in me.

In my Father's house are many mansions: if it were not so, I would have told you. I go to prepare a place for you.

And if I go and prepare a place for you, I will come again, and receive you unto myself; that where I am, there ye may be also.

And whither I go ye know and the way ye know.

John 14: 1-6

O death, where is thy sting?
O grave, where is thy victory?

I Corinthians 15:55

He will wipe every tear from their eyes. There will be no more death or mourning or crying or pain, for the old order of things has passed away.
Revelations 21:4 (NIV)

MIRRORS

Romance of partying and night life
Has faded into sepia tone
my partner's response is now silenced
I find myself dancing alone.

I frequently choose to recall
Days laced with laughter and song
Spirit impassioned with living
Carefree and physically strong.

Life we now share is more tender
Idyllic romance more true
Times when I whisper, "I love you, "
Gently he mumbles, "Love you, too."

Frances Darby

TO FATHOM HIM

To Him whose life spans all the time,
And time that still must be.
I clasp my hands, and close my eyes,
I bow on bended knee.

I plunge beneath His gracious love,
I cannot understand,
How God could place a worth on me
And keep me in His hand.

God is!
My, what those words embrace!
They fairly shout, "Because He is,
All else remains in place."

He whose life has spanned all of time
And time before time was;
Guides the destiny of my soul,
And lifts me to His love.

Kenneth V. Francart

Ordained in the Southern Baptist ministry, Rev.
Francart, Memphis, Tennessee, has been involved with
religious writing and counseling. This poem was written
shortly after open-heart surgery.

REMEMBERED

Two tiny graves, side by side
Small pieces of this earth marked with
with little stones bearing names and dates.
So small: our babies, our loves,
our children, our future--
                His baby brother and sister.
                Their grandchildren.
So small
So full of love
So precious.

Gwen Vescovo

In 1975 the Vescovo family lost Anthony Earnest Vescovo, at two and one-half months; in 1981 they lost Jenny Rebecca Vescovo when she was one day old. The above poem was part of the expressions of love and faith the family put together.

Gwen Vescovo celebrated the joy her children brought to her. In a letter to Anthony, she says "... I thank God for every second I had with you. I pray that I may always remember the beauty of your birth and the joy of your short life."

Their son Christian was born in 1972. Another daughter Mary Kathryn was born in 1982. Both are healthy and happy. Gwen, whose family are members of Holy Rosary Catholic Church, Memphis, TN, was a facilitator of a Parents Experiencing Perinatal Death support group for many years. She is a telephone friend of the Compassionate Friends support group.

SIGNATURE

Your signature on old letters
flowed from your pen
as strong and sure as your faith in me
yet as frail and finite
as the flesh and blood
of a human life.

The indelible shape reminds me still
of how your life once mingled with mine
and how I strove to learn from you
the instrument which has become
as essential to me as breathing.

Though your flute is silent
and your pen still
your signature pulses through me now
as alive as a heartbeat
as timeless as music.

Sometimes
for a fleeting moment
in the awesome hush before the downbeat
I hear your voice
I wait for your baton:
Sometimes
I feel the twinkle in your eyes
resting on me.

*In memory of my teacher, Geoffrey Winzer Gilbert, who left
his signature not only in letters, but in lives.*

Rebecca T. Googe, Professor of Music at Lambuth College,
Jackson, Tennessee

CAMEO BROOCH

In Memory of Mother
Ruth Burnette Bolin

Treasured cameo of your precious form--
My brooch--it fastens round my memories
Here enshrined, like a cloak; memories
Frayed from frequent use bring warmth
Like woolen comforts tucked around small
Shoulders on bitter winter nights--your
Tireless, loving mother's touch bestowed
As well creative cures to nurse the hurt
Or sick wild birds and dogs and cats.
I long to wrap my arms around you--
Gently kiss your brow--but memories spring
Forward toward today across your granite
Stone--kneeling I touch cold, cold
Clay--yet feel my cloak as warm...

Burnette Bolin Benedict

Author of *Kinship,* Grandmother Earth Chapbook Merit Winner 1995, Burnette Benedict is from Knoxville, Tennessee.

BEFORE THE SUNSET
(FOR REYNOLDS)

You went before the sun sank in the sky...
I heard the ragged rasping of your breath
And wondered why we mortals have to die
And who has jurisdiction over death.

And I can not erase you from my heart...
Those times when rain beat patterns in our minds,
For we were close together from the start...
Poured down a gristmill that the miller grinds.

Today I hear one lonely mockingbird
Singing your dirge across the August winds,
And I find comfort in the Holy Word...
Believing that our union never ends.

And so I give you back to earth and stone
While half of me walks through the mist alone.

Frieda Beasley Dorris

This poem was read at the Memorial Service of Reynolds O. Dorris: November 29, 1912--August 9, 1994. Both were members of the Catholic Church of the Resurrection, Memphis, Tennessee, Frieda is an Honorary Member of the Poetry Society of Tennessee.

GRANDMA'S ROSE GARDEN

Grandma is tending her rose garden
a smudged work apron
a straw hat that's molting
red scratches on arms
hands work-roughened.

She rests for a moment
leaning down to smell a rose;
she smiles to herself
takes a deep breath
and sighs.

Grandma snips several blooms
Pastel rosebuds of perfect form
to bring inside
to set in a vase
for placement beside her Bible.

She prepares a tea service for two
a cup for herself
to be filled
the other
not filled.

Grandma opens her worn Bible
reads the 23rd Psalm
then closes her eyes to rest;
to reminisce
with her soul at peace.

The rosebuds
beside Grandma's Bible
silently unfold.

Neal Hogenbirk, Waretown, New Jersey
A retired forester, writer and photographer.

YOU CAN COME HOME NOW

Mama,
You've gone home now
and
you are happy.
You prayed for it,
asked forgiveness,
then passively waited
on God.
You said your good-byes,
caught up on your reading,
finished your work.
You waited on God
and he said,
"Naomi, I'm ready;
you can come home now;
angels will show you the way."

Joyously you took angel's hands,
soared out of the rainy
earth's atmosphere
toward heaven's
shining radiance.
You met your Savior,
greeted mama and papa,
sisters and brothers,
your life's companion,
myriad friends
and familiar saints,
and suddenly you knew
you had a new body.

It was well, gloriously well,
wouldn't ever be sick again!

Mama, I can't imagine
all the things they showed you,
can't imagine
what you're doing now
yet
you are happy, fulfilled,
content at home,
eagerly participating
in heaven's offerings.

Ruth Thomas

A retired English teacher, Ruth Thomas, Humbolt, Tennessee, is a Christian writer and poet and active in the United Methodist Women's Organization.

HER GOLDEN THREAD

for Eve and Bill Hatchett

He slipped away but left a golden thread...
He loved her with a love beyond compare.
He left no deeds nor words of love unsaid--
The roses that he sent still linger there

      Where they prayed
      together
      she now prays
      alone

For comfort through each long and lonely night
She has to live without his loving touch.
Yet part of him is sewn within her soul...
He slipped away but left a golden thread.

FBC

GRANDMA SINGS
EVERY EASTER

I thought I saw her in the crowd--
white hair, wearing glasses
a smile echoing last Easter
when she really was there...

Other golden age grandmothers
looked toward the choir remembering services
when they had not been alone--
trying to keep the clean-faced and crisply-dressed
boys and girls they had brought with them
crisp, and above all, quiet.
For almost a hundred Easter mornings
Grandma had sung these songs
and heard these words.
"Lo, He is not in the tomb."
"Christ the Lord has risen today! "
"Hallelujah! Hallelujah!"
I join the chorus as tears turn to joy.
Easter is not the time to mourn,
nor is there any reason to.
Grandma is somewhere singing
"Hallelujah! Hallelujah!"
    Forever. Amen.

FBC

Be strong and courageous. Do not be afraid...The Lord himself goes before you and will be with you; he will never leave you nor forsake you. Do not be afraid; do not be discouraged."
Deuteronomy 31:6, 8 (NIV)

A SPECIAL BLESSING

Louise Gill

Shortly after my retirement when I had just gotten into a normal routine, God stirred the nest. My husband Doyne's father had lived alone for twenty years. After his wife died, Walter became detached from his two sons and their families and moved to his farm. He grew a garden, collected junk, and kept to himself. He had no telephone and would not respond to mail. The only contact we had would be to drive 130 miles and try to locate him. Sometimes we'd catch him there and at others it was impossible to know where he was. My husband's younger brother, Gene, lived about ten miles away and occasionally Walter would go to visit his family. We could call a neighbor down the road to check on him.

One day we received a call that Walter was ill and we should try to get him to let us help. Cancer was discovered when a shaving cut did not heal. Walter was driving himself fifty miles into Little Rock for treatment. Gene was unable to get him to come to his house. My husband took time off from work to go to him, but we were unable to convince him to go with us or with Gene. He would not come live with us because he wanted to be as near to his doctor as possible. Because we knew he was not able to continue driving himself, I began driving over to the farm and taking him to the doctor and then driving back to Memphis.

Finally, I was able to persuade him to go home with me and stay between treatments. This routine went on for several weeks. He still would not agree to go to stay more than two days at the time.

One day as I was praying, seeking God's will, I felt the urgency to go and bring him home with me. Walter was at Gene's all by himself. His daughter-in-law was in New Jersey taking care of her daughter and a new grand baby. Gene was at work all day.

I could not get him to come home until I told him, "God had sent me to get you, and you better go or we are both in big trouble." With that he got into the car and did not say a word all the way back to Memphis.

This was the beginning of a miracle. I got his medical records transferred to an oncologist in Memphis. With all of our children gone, he had a choice of rooms. He chose the smallest room upstairs, the one across the hall from our bedroom. I put a big chair by the window. and he enjoyed looking out at the birds, squirrels, trees and plants.

When he recovered enough from each chemo treatment we would go for frequent drives to the produce stores. We spent hours talking. Assuming responsibility for his care brought us closer and closer.

Little by little, Walter also began to develop a relationship with his son and with his grandchildren and their spouses. At Christmas we gathered in the living room for the traditional reading of the Christmas story and took turns telling what Christ meant to us. He had not spent many holidays with his children, so this was a new experience for him.

We took turns praying; and to our surprise, Granddaddy began to pray. What a blessing this was to all of us! We had never head him pray before even though we had prayed aloud at his bedside many times. God is so good!

Our relationship developed until I grew to love him as my own father. We were alone most evenings, and we talked, laughed, cried and had a wonderful time together. I grew to love baseball because he was a big fan. We listened to the World Series on the radio together.

By the next November, Walter was so weak that we realized his time was very short. Gene and his family came over for this. He was so heavily sedated he hardly realized they were there.

On December 5, 1985, about 3:00 p.m., he quietly slipped away. When he realized that he was taking his last breath, we embraced, praised God and wept. Then we realized what a treasure we had. God had been so real and close to us through out this entire time.

Sometimes I felt hurt and anger because I didn't have more time with him, and then I would feel guilty that I could have done more. But then I thanked God for allowing us this special blessing of getting to know my husband's father.

Walter accepted Jesus as his savior during this time, and I know he is in heaven now.

Louise Gill is an member of Bellevue Baptist Church, Memphis, Tennessee, where she has taught the Senior High Youth Sunday School for 35 years. She has taught in Bible Study Fellowship and leads seminars for various women's groups.

GUIDELINES FOR GRIEF

*To every thing there is a season, and a time to
every purpose under the heaven:*

*A time to be born, and a time to die; a time to
plant, and a time to pluck up that which is planted;*

*A time to kill, and a time to heal; a time to
break down, and a time to build up;*

*A time to weep, and a time to laugh; a time to
mourn, and a time to dance;*

*A time to cast away stones, and a time to gather
stones together; a time to embrace, and a time to
refrain from embracing;*

*A time to get, and a time to lose; a time to keep,
and a time to cast away;*

*A time to rend, and a time to sew; a time to
keep silence, and a time to speak;*

*A time to love, and a time to hate; a time of
war, and a time of peace.*

Ecclesiastes 3:1-8

In this you greatly rejoice, though now for a little while you may have had to suffer grief in all kinds of trials. These have come so that your faith--of greater worth than gold, which perishes even though refined by fire-- may be proved genuine and may result in praise, glory and honor when Jesus Christ is revealed. 1 Peter 1:6, 7 (NIV)

WAITING AND HOPING

Dr. J. Herbert Hester

There is not one of us who has not come to a time when our strength seemed to be inadequate. The strength that we have relied upon so often in the past seems suddenly to grow weak and frail.

God through His prophet, Isaiah, clearly spoke to us about these times. **"Even youths shall faint and be weary, and the young men shall utterly fail; but they that wait upon the Lord shall renew their strength; they shall mount up with wings as eagles; they shall run, and not be weary, and they shall walk, and not faint."** (Isaiah 40:30-31)

Even the strongest of us grow tired, weary, and exhausted. We reach those moments when physically, emotionally, spiritually, or perhaps all three, we have come to what many would refer to as "the end of our rope." We have no more strength. When those times come for the believer, God tells us there is hope; there is a plan that God has made for us. The answer lies in not depending upon our own strength, but placing ourselves in the position that we are living in the strength of our Heavenly Father. This is described in Isaiah 40:31 where in the King's James Version we read **"they that wait upon the Lord shall renew their strength."** That same phrase is translated in the New International Version as "but those that hope in the Lord will renew their strength." The dual translation of one Hebrew word by the two words "wait" and "hope" helps us to understand how we can apply God's strength to our lives.

The idea of *waiting* does not carry with it a passive existence where one simply retreats into his own self and waits patiently for God to do something. *Waiting* is not passive at all; as a matter of fact, it shows great energy.

Waiting has an eagerness about it. We might describe it like the farmer who waits eagerly for the seeds that he has planted to become the harvest that he anticipates. The word for "wait" comes from a Hebrew word that means "to wind" or "to twist." As we "wait upon the Lord," we are actively entwining our lives with that of our Heavenly Father, so that every part of us is closely associated with some part of our Heavenly Father. It is the idea of a rope made up of many separate strands. Separately, these little strands are easily broken, but when they are woven together, they suddenly become part of a bigger whole, which is now strong. This is the kind of strength that is important to us. It becomes God's unfailing strength, which is available to us at times when we feel faint and weary. It comes to us as we actively learn to *wait* upon Him. It touches us as we come to those hours when we are sick, when we have a loved one who is facing terrible trials in his life or perhaps when we have lost someone to death that we love very much. So when the weary times come and the dark hours are upon us, we realize that we rely upon His strength and not our own.

One of the greatest attributes of our waiting actively on the Lord is that it constantly produces hope within us, a hope that is constantly renewed in our heart telling us that we will never be outside of God's care as we walk day to day through life's various experiences. It also reminds us that there is a future for us beyond life here on earth. It is the "blessed hope" of the Second Coming of Jesus Christ as Paul referred to it. It is our hope of an eternal home in heaven with Him.

Our hope reminds us that on the day that we placed our faith and trust in Jesus Christ, our faith became active. Believing with all of our heart that He is the Son of God and receiving Him as Savior and Lord provides for us the precious gift of eternal life in heaven with God. This belief and trust allows Him to take care of us on a day-to-day basis, no matter what the everyday circumstances may be. Knowing in the darkest hours of discouragement, and even death, God has completed a great work through His Son Jesus Christ which He continually offers to us; His presence here on earth and His glorious heaven in the days ahead. It is our faith that allows us to see someday that everything God has promised us will come to completion.

This kind of waiting and hoping is seen strongly in a man of faith. A man of faith often soars like an eagle, often runs because of the presence of God without weariness, but most importantly the man of faith walks with God day by day.

The real test of our faith is not seen in those moments where God allows us to fly and soar like an eagle. The real test of our faith is not seen in those times when God allows us to mount up and run with strength that seems like it will never end. The real test of our faith is seen as we walk day by day through the every day circumstances of life, and yes death, and come out on the other side with victory. Our everyday faith walk reveals our true character.

To "wait upon the Lord" means to respond in faith to the great message of His abundant life here on earth and His future coming for His children. The understanding of such a message goes far beyond anything else we will ever encounter in life. Jesus' coming lies in the future. The response of faith today makes its benefits available to us now. You see, faith is not merely the means by which we achieve the victory. The truth is that Faith Is The Victory.

Dr. Hester is Senior Pastor at Colonial Baptist Church, Memphis, Tennessee. This is an exherpt from the memorial service for Raymond McCarty, first president of the Poetry Society of Tennessee.

"I WILL NEVER LEAVE YOU..."

Mary Ann Piercey

I had been privileged to be in Memphis and spend quality time with my parents the last few years of their lives. What a blessing for me!

The death of my father in 1989 and my mother two years later ended their ill health and pain. I was amazed at the strength God gave me to do what had to be done.

But when it was over, I felt a sense of loss I could hardly bear. We had been very close. I had cared for one and then the other while they were sick and *now they were gone!*

I turned to the scripture and found Hebrews 13:5. "...for He hath said, "I will never leave you, nor forsake you." and "When anxiety was great within me, your consolation brought joy to my soul." Psalm 94:19 (NIV)

In addition to the help and support I felt from the scriptures, I followed a friend's suggestion and became a volunteer at Methodist Hospital Central with her. I found that by helping others and continuing my devotional life, my grief began to lift and I could see the gifts and blessings I had received from my parents. Thanks to God who cares for me and gave me something to share!

A member of the Prayer Group at Colonial Park United Methodist Church, Memphis, Tennessee, where her husband is Senior Pastor, Mary Ann Piercey participates actively in the life of the church. She is a pink lady volunteer at Methodist Hospital and also co-chairs the Bazaar Committee of the Methodist Hospital Auxiliary.

*But seek ye first the kingdom of God and his righteousness;
and all these things shall be added unto you.* Matthew 6:33.

MORE THAN MEMORIES

Sally Eudaly

One of my memories is of the precious few minutes
we sat together in our car, my beloved Woodie and I. He
was in the back seat, I was in the front. But we were so
together! In one month's time, he had changed from a
healthy, six-foot-one, active man into an emaciated, pain-
ridden invalid; but he still looked like Prince Charming to
me.

Several hours before we had gone through a
monumental ordeal. He, so weak he could barely hold his
razor, had managed to shave himself with great slashes at his
face without cutting anything but whiskers. The two of us
had toiled until we had dressed him in sport coat and slacks
(no robe and pajamas tonight). We had toiled again to get
him into the back seat of the car so I could drive to the
elegant home of his boss who had prepared a party in his
honor.

As we had drove up the driveway, big double doors
at the front of the lovely home were thrown open. The men
with whom he had worked poured out to greet him. They
laughed, whistled, teased, and raised him on their shoulders
to carry him inside to the bright lights, pretty secretaries
and wives, and wonderful food. For the first time in days
he was able to eat as the guests took turns gathering around
him. During those few hours at that party we forgot our
helplessness and felt normal again.

Now, having been hugged and loved and returned to our home, we sat there in our familiar driveway in our car, still aglow. It was as if there really was no cancer or threatening desolation.

"Let's just sit here a minute," Woodie said. It was quiet, dark. The lights were on inside the house because our teenage daughter was there. We were so together, he in the back seat, I in the front.

Woodie broke the silence, "I am going to lick this thing!"

Tears poured out of my eyes, but he could not see them in the dark. "I couldn't live without you," I managed to say.

But I did! Woodie died a month later.

There is worldy mercy in the custom of burning the widow on her husband's funeral pyre. It frees her from the intense pain of loss when a great wonder has been known and then ripped away. I needed to know that God has a companionship that can never be ripped away in store for me. I needed to concentrate on the glimmer that the wonder of my life with Woodie had given me. It gave me a picture of being the bride of Christ. "But my God shall supply all your need according to his riches in glory by Christ Jesus." Philippians 4:19.

After Woodie's death it was hard to feel much communion with God. I definitely turned to my Bible and continued to pray, but all I really wanted was my life with Woodie. God did what He promised in Philippians 4:13: "I can do all things through Christ which strengtheneth me." I could see His provision even when I was not obedient, but I still felt emptiness and an ache for the person who was gone. I even felt rejection, as if Woodie were hiding and did not want to be with me.

Now, nearly twenty years later, I have eyes to see more clearly. God has been standing outside my door, just as I have often done with my own children, guarding me, ready to intervene if necessary. His purpose, as He watches, is to bless me with understanding of a love that will never be permanent or satisfied outside of Him.

I knew God's offer for putting Jesus first. "And everyone that hath forsaken houses, or brethren, or sisters, or father, or mother, or wife, or children, or lands, for my name's sake shall receive an hundred fold, and shall inherit everlasting life." Matthew 19:29. But everlasting life was far off. I could not forsake Woodie for Jesus. I held on to him as hard as I could. Woodie was *taken away*! I did not deserve the obvious blessings I received: a second husband who is godly and a part of a three-way marriage, he and I and Jesus; interactions with friends, five married children, and fourteen and one-half grandchildren; work that makes me feel worthwhile; good health. "All things work together for good to them that love God." Romans 8:28

I believe the reward for forsaking is prioritizing. The hundred-fold blessing is eternal, not ephemeral. It is the learning I will take with me to the nursing home when I am a hundred. It will be more than memories; it will be praising God for what can never be ripped away: God is there. The Bible is real. All of us are sinners. It is as just as easy to find something to praise as is to find things to cry about. It is not what we *do* that counts; it's what we *learn* about God's righteousness. There is always the joy of work in God's kingdom. As long as we allow it, the Holy Spirit will teach us.

Sally Eudaly has retired from teaching elementary students in a Memphis City School. She has taught Bible Study Fellowship and a variety of Sunday School classes at Colonial Park United Methodist Church, Memphis, Tennessee.

Commit to the Lord what ever you do, and your plans will succeed. Proverbs 16:3 (NIV)

LISTEN FOR HIS CALLING

Blanche Boren

As servants for our Lord Jesus Christ, we must pray daily for Him to show us what He would have us do. If we stay tuned in, He may call us at the most expected times.

On a recent Sunday, I was getting dressed for church when my phone rang. My friend Mary called to let me know that the husband of our friend Dora was given only hours to live. As soon as I hung up, I began to pray for Dora and her Christian husband that God was calling home. As I prayed I began to feel that God was calling me to go to the hospital to be with Dora and her family. I kept thinking of excuses not to go. I didn't have enough time to go before church and maybe they did not want intruders during their time of sorrow.

But God kept sending me the message to go, and finally I went. When I arrived at the intensive care waiting room the family was in his room. I started writing a note. But before I could leave, my friend Dora and her daughter came out and saw me.

Dora hugged me, clinging to me saying, "Thank you for coming. I had used all my strength and God sent you for me to lean on and use your strength. Thank you so much." And I almost didn't go!

Silently I thanked God for using me. Then I prayed with her, asking God to give her a new strength, and keep her in his care.

Dora insisted that I be with the family when the doctor told the family that he had died. Praise God! I was able to minister to the family and be a witness for Him.

"God sent you to me at this time because I needed you," Dora told me as we prayed together. Praise be to God for the opportunity to share his love.

And we know that in all things God works for the good of those who love him, who have been called according to his purpose. Romans 8:28 (NIV)

AS WE FORGIVE

Earline W. Duncan

A Christian's life is filled with many little vignettes and yet each is the part of a larger picture. When the downside of life hits one who loves God and serves him, he or she knows that there is some good that comes out of trying times. Many Christians can share stories of times when a bad situation led to a happy event. Every aspect of our lives is important to God when we love Him. We must remember that there is nothing that we experience that is not used for the betterment of the total picture of our lives. When the rain comes, remember that we need it to make flowers grow. The same thing is true with the rains of life.

My brother's death was sudden and violent. It was difficult for me to see this as "good." During this period, I told his wife, who had killed him, that she was in my prayers. She said that meant much to her. The fact is that it left the door open for a family relationship with my brother's children. With the help of the Lord, I was able to forgive her. Today my brother's children feel the love that only comes from a warm and friendly family relationship. Not only did this help me to grow but now I am able to help other victims of violent crimes see the merit of forgiving those who trespass against them. REMEMBER: All things work together for good to those that love God.

Earline Duncan is a Critical Thinking teacher in Memphis City Schools at Lester Elementary and is active in St. James A. M. E. Church, Memphis, Tennessee.

EVEN BEFORE WE ASK

Betty Ford Cowden

Last summer, while visiting relatives in Memphis, Tennessee, two sisters-in-law and I spent a very pleasant Saturday morning going to yard sales. I found a well-used paperback copy of Billy Graham's book, *Angels: God's Secret Agents,* and paid ten cents for it. While in the car waiting for the others, I read the last paragraph.

> The Scripture says there is a time to be
> born and a time to die. And when my time
> to die comes an angel will be there to comfort
> me. He will give me peace and joy even
> at that most critical hour, and usher me into
> the presence of God, and I will dwell with
> the Lord forever. Thank God for the ministry
> of His blessed angels![1]

That afternoon when I returned to my home in Batesville, Arkansas, the phone was ringing. A cousin from New Hampshire was calling to tell me that my beloved cousin, Mabel, in Oklahoma City had fallen and had died instantly. I have lost two husbands and my father so I understand the pain we feel, but this seemed so hard to accept.

Broken hearted, I hurried out to my garden. I said, "Lord, I need the comfort that can only come from you." Immediately a scripture from Psalms 91:11 came to my mind, "For he shall give his angels charge over thee, to keep thee in all thy ways."

I replied, "That's good, Lord, but it's not enough."

An almost audible voice responded, "I gave you comfort today, even before you knew you needed it."

In my mind's eye I could see that last paragraph from the little book on angels. I said, "Yes, Lord, Mabel had an angel with her at the time of her death and she has already been escorted into Your very presence. I came back inside my home with a heart filled with peace. Now I really understand the words of the old spiritual "I looked over Jordan and what did I see? Comin' for to carry me home."

Thank you, Lord, that you understand us so well and answer our prayers even before we ask.

Betty Ford Cowden is a retired elementary teacher and teaches Sunday School classes at Faith-Hopewell Cumberland Presbyterian, Batesville, Arkansas.

[1] *Angels: God's Secret Agents*, Billy Graham, Pocket Book edition 1977, Pocket Books a division of Simon & Schuster, Inc. NY., NY. Used with permission of Word Publishing.

RE-ORIENTING GRIEF

Patricia W. Smith

I was born into a rather unique family: small town, family funeral home owned and run by my grandfather. Many of my earliest memories are of playing hide-and-seek in the display rooms and watching my grandfather and his technicians at work. Despite what some would call a grisly profession, he was one of the most up-beat men I have ever known. Though not a go-to-church-every-Sunday person, he had a deep and abiding faith in God and God's word.

The first Bible verses he taught me were the lines from John 16:1-6 which include the familiar "In my Father's house are many mansions...." "Remember," he would tell me, "death is not the end of life but the beginning of life with God and should be a celebration, not a time of weeping and wailing and gnashing of teeth. Our life on this earth is only a prelude to that greater life to come."

"Why did Uncle Johnny have to die?" I asked. My Uncle Johnny was sixteen when he was killed by a drunk driver.

"God gave man free will and sometimes people make improper decisions that result in someone's death. On those occasions God grieves too, but He also rejoices that one of His has come to Him. I'm not telling you not to grieve, but to grieve in a positive way, to rejoice with God."

I have tried very hard to keep to this philosophy of death and grieving, although at times it has been difficult. It is so much easier to be ego-centered when a dear one dies. We hear, "I don't want to go on living without him," or "My life will never be the same," or "It's not fair," or "I don't deserve this," or "Why did God do this to me?" This is ego-centered grieving.

Since World War II, the Mom and Pop funeral home has gone the way of the Mom and Pop grocery store and has been replaced by what I call supermarket funeral factories. No longer is the funeral director a friend there to help us through a difficult time; now he is a big businessman looking to his bottom line. You hear, "But surely you want to do the right thing." and "That is simply not the best." and "Might I suggest that..." These people encourage and depend on ego-centered grief. They want to make you feel guilty if you do not purchase the top-of-the-line merchandise for the funeral, when you, the grieving, are guilty of nothing.

To grieve is normal, just as it is to breathe. Let us strive to grieve in a positive manner by including God in our grieving. Let us celebrate the passage of a dear one to a life everlasting with God. We have to live with the funeral factories just as we have to deal with the supermarkets today, but we can try to make the services more God-centered. For the memorial service select God-centered hymns such as "A Mighty Fortress Is Our God." Request that appropriate memorials be made in place of flowers. Insist that a minister run the service, not a funeral director, or better yet have the funeral in your church. Have family members participate in the service, reading the Bible passages, singing or whatever seems proper to you and your minister. Most of all, keep the atmosphere up-beat and celebratory.

When we replace ego-centered grief with God-centered grief we are healthier both spiritually and emotionally. It can be done.

Patricia Smith is a retired chemist and a communicant of Good Shepherd Episcopal Church, Memphis, Tennessee.

We love him, because he first loved us. I John 4:19

WHAT CAN I DO?

There are many times in life when we are faced with grief--critical illness, death of a loved one, divorce or a disabling accident. Because we love, we suffer loss. Because God loves us, He can help us deal with our situation.

HOW YOU CAN HELP THE DYING PERSON DEAL WITH GRIEF

Explore your own feelings about death, so you can better understand how the dying person feels. Who are you? What is God's role in death? Where does our control begin and end. How would you feel if it were you instead?

Respect the right of the patient to handle death in his or her own way. But be there as a positive support. Go along with denial (but don't reinforce it). Remember you are not the target. Don't take anger personally. Try to help the person think through the pain instead of lashing out. Let the person grieve, and don't be afraid to cry also. But move on to happy memories if possible as soon as you have allowed the dying person time for expression.

Accept the person's forthcoming death and be open about it. Think of ways to make the last days more peaceful. Help meet physical needs--see that pain is relieved, run errands, etc. Also listen and watch for clues to unspoken emotional needs. Show you really care and are available.

Pray with the patient for God's presence and for the strength and assurance only the Holy Spirit can give. If he or she is too angry to pray with you, pray when you are alone. Do not avoid mentioning God, but rather talk about some of your own beliefs without preaching. Your faith and your actions are the most effective witness.

HELPING THE FAMILY

During the period of dying, family members may also experience denial and anger toward the dying person. Help them understand these feelings and those of the dying person, so the healing process can begin. Moreover, listen when they want to express grief before and after the loved one's death. Tension can be relieved by sharing a sweet memory about the loved one.

Prepare a child before a loved one dies if possible. Talk about death when the subject arises naturally--such as, when a pet dies. When a siren sounds in their presence, teach children to say a prayer for those in trouble.

Children may feel anger or fear being abandoned by someone they had depended upon. Sometimes there may be confusion about what has happened or even guilt that they may have caused death to happen. Most authorities believe that children should be allowed to share in family grief and to attend services with the rest of the family if they want to. You can help children accept death by answering all questions simply and truthfully and by helping them express their feelings. Reassure them that death is not their fault, and that they will be taken care of. Be a positive, loving example for them.

PERSONAL GRIEVING

Accept the grief without using it as a crutch. Do not hold in the tears. Cry alone or with others. Talk about it. Share your grief with your family and with close friends. Talk about good memories of the loved one. Helping other family members or friends deal with the grief is the best way to deal with your own.

Pray for deliverance from guilt feelings. You can not change anything now. You probably did the best you could at the time. If you did make mistakes, can you imagine your loved one wanting you to dwell on them? If God can forgive you, you can surely do the same.

Accept your understanding of the death, for the

time being. You have probably asked "why?" over and over and have finally realized that there is no acceptable answer. But you probably have some small degree of understanding. Pray that you will be able to get through one day at a time. No matter how deep your sorrow, you are not alone. Others have been there and will help share your load if you will let them. Do not deny them the opportunity. Join a support group of others who are dealing with their grief. Don't be afraid to call on friends. Some of your relationships with people may change. Seek out those friends or even acquaintances that have given you evidence of their strong religious faith by their life style. Some friends might be embarrassed by your presence at first, but they will get over it if you will ask for their help in specific ways instead of just feeling sorry for yourself.

Channel grief into creative energy by helping others. Sharing someone else's burden will lighten yours and keep you from isolating yourself.

Take care of your health and keep busy with meaningful activities. At first you may feel that you don't care, but eventually you will realize that you are important too. During stressful situations your body needs nourishment more than ever. The bio-chemical changes brought by exercise can help with depression and with sleeping problems.

Do not make major decisions. It is not a good idea to sell your house, change jobs or move across the country until you have had time to weigh all of the consequences.

Record your thoughts in a journal, even if you are not inclined toward writing. No one has to read what you have written except you. It helps release your feelings and records your progress. To get started, read what others have written about dealing with death and record your reactions. Try writing poetry. After you have expressed your deepest grief, end each poem with a blessing you received through faith.

Get professional help if needed. Do not allow grief to continue to cripple your life. There comes a time to stop crying and to live again. Sometimes just a few sessions with a trained counselor will help you to resolve the anger, guilt, and despair that keep you from functioning in every day life.

Take advantage of your church's activities. If you don't have a church, visit religious services with some of your friends. This is the time to find out who you really are and what you want your relationship with God to be. Words from *The Holy Bible* and from hymns can be very comforting. Build upon your faith. As time passes and your faith grows, you will find your anger is channeled toward finding or strengthening your own special relationship with God.

FBC

RAINBOW WISHES

May Our God
   surround you
    with circles of love
     that you see only
       green, gold and purple
       in the grayest cloud
    the sparkle
  in each raindrop
and feel his presence
around you
each and every day.

Frances Brinkley Cowden
from *Purpose Magazine*

THOUGHTS AT GRANDMOTHER'S FUNERAL

She will never die.

She will wait in country lanes with open arms.

Through the mists of twilight
we will hear her wavering voice singing off-key
"Amazing Grace," "The Old Rugged Cross," and
"I'm Going to Rock Around the Clock Tonight."

When we are discouraged and hungry
she will offer warm cookies, a hug,
and a piece of fried chicken.

When we ache she will tuck us into bed
and whisper,
"Everything is going to be all right."

When we go outside on frosty mornings
she will call to us to come back inside
for a coat, gloves, scarf, and galoshes.

She will continue to admonish and advise:
"Say Yes, Ma'am." "Smile." "Be sweet."
"A penny saved is a penny earned."
"Just do the best you can."

She will walk with us in our gardens.
She will point to new plants
that have descended from seeds
brought from over the water
by her grandmothers,
or their grandmothers,
or before.

She asks that we in turn pass on our heritage
to our children and grandchildren
and to all those who come afterward.

Grandmothers endure and prevail.

Malra Treece

Malra Treece is Professor Emeritus, College of Business and
Economics, University of Memphis.   She is a charter
member of Colonial Park United Methodist Church,
Memphis, Tennessee.

Weeping may endure for a night, but joy cometh in the morning. Psalms 30:5

THE COMING OF WINTER

The snow falls unexpectedly. I thought
the time was May or June, or August at
the latest. Winds blow cold upon my face,
recalling autumn warmth, the blessing of
the summer sun, the promises of spring
so softly whispered by the gentle breeze
of morning. Yet for everything there is
a season. This I know but fight against
unceasingly. I would not want the leaves,
now brown and comfortable beneath the snow,
to once again be brightly clinging to
the tree, which spreads its bare black limbs against
the sky. I'll walk with gratitude across
the frozen fields where I ran joyfully
in early spring when they were green and gold.

Malra Treece

ACKNOWLEDGMENTS

Appreciation for prayers from friends at Colonial Park United Methodist Church and from the Memphis Tuesday Evening Women's Group of Bible Study Fellowship and for guidance from the Holy Spirit in the completion of this book.

Editorial Assistance from: Elaine Nunnally Davis, Gladys Ellis, Carolyn Taylor and Blanche Boren
Permission for use of his illustration from
Dr. Leonard Sweet
Permission for the use of the quote from *Angels: God's Secret Agents* by Reverend Billy Graham
by Word Publishing Company
Photography by Neal Hogenbirk

Some of the work in this book appeared previously in *Tennessee Voices, Purpose Magazine, View From a Mississippi River Cotton Sack, Justice or Mercy, Morning At East Elementary School*

§§

Readers may submit personal experiences for consideration in the forthcoming

Person to Person to God

a collection of mediations and testimonies on the power of prayer and the fruits of the Holy Spirit scheduled to be published by 1998.

§§

A collection of angel experiences, *Messengers of Love: in His Image,* is scheduled for publication November, 1996

PUBLICATIONS BY
GRANDMOTHER EARTH

1-884289-01-0 *VIEW FROM A MISSISSIPPI RIVER COTTON SACK*--Frances Brinkley Cowden, coil , 1993, $9.95
1-884289- 03-7 ED 2--cloth, 1994, $19.95
1-884289-00-2 *TAKE TIME TO LAUGH*--Eve Braden Hatchett, staple, 1993, $7.95
1-884289-04-5 *BUTTERFLIES AND UNICORNS* ED 4, Frances Brinkley Cowden and Eve Braden Hatchett, paper, 1994, $8.50
1-884289-O6-1 *TO LOVE A WHALE*--Frances Brinkley Cowden, Editor, paper, 1995, $11.95
1-884289-07-X *ASHES TO OAK*, Shirley Rounds Schirz, staple, 1995, $6.95
1-884289-08-8 *KINSHIP*, Burnette Bolin Benedict, staple, 1995, $7.95
1-884289-09-6 *GRANDMOTHER EARTH I: 1995*
1-884289-14-2 *GRANDMOTHER EARTH II: 1996*
1-884289-16-9, *GRANDMOTHER EARTH III: 1997* Prize-winning poems and prose, $11.95 each.
SUBSCRIPTION, $10 per year
1-884289-17-7, Jack Daniel, SOUTHERN RAILWAY: FROM STEVENSON TO MEMPHIS, paper, 1996, limited edition, $24.95

LIFE PRESS

1-884289-05-3 *MOTHERS OF JESUS*, Elaine Nunnally Davis, paper, 1994, $15.95
1-884289-11-8 *EVE'S FRUIT*, Elaine Nunnally Davis, paper, 1995, $14.95
1-884289-12-6 *BLOOM WHERE YOU ARE TRANSPLANTED*, Geraldine Ketchum Crow, paper, 1996, $11.95